D1546874

THE 1980s

ISBN 0-634-04035-9

HAL•LEONARD®
CORPORATION

7777 W. BLUEMOUND RD. P.O. BOX 13819 MILWAUKEE, WI 53213

Visit Hal Leonard Online at
www.halleonard.com

CONTENTS

Caught Up in You

Words and Music by Frank Sullivan, Jim Peterik, Jeff Carlisi and Don Barnes

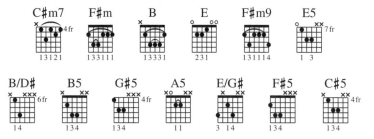

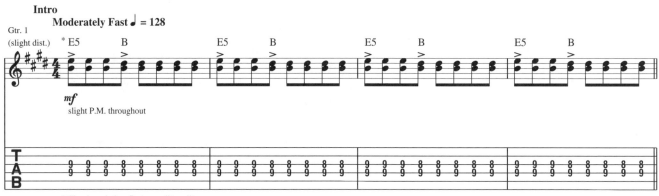

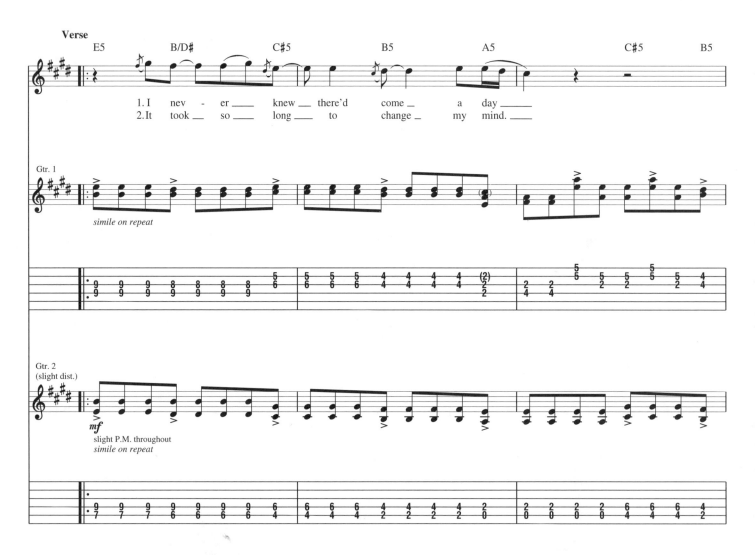

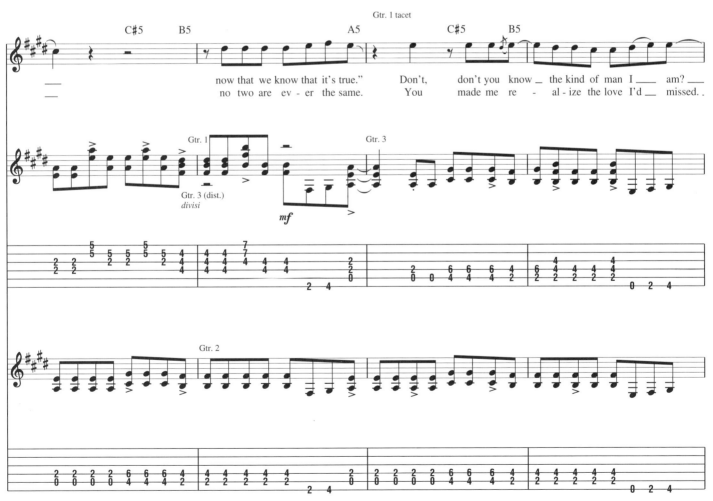

No,   said I'd nev - er fall in love a - gain. ___ But it's real   and the feel -
So   hot,   love ___ I could - n't quite re - sist.   When it's right   the light _

-ing   comes _ shin - ing   through. _____   I'm so   caught up   in you, __
___ just   comes _ shin - ing   through. _____   I'm so   caught up in you, __

* composite arrangement

Chorus

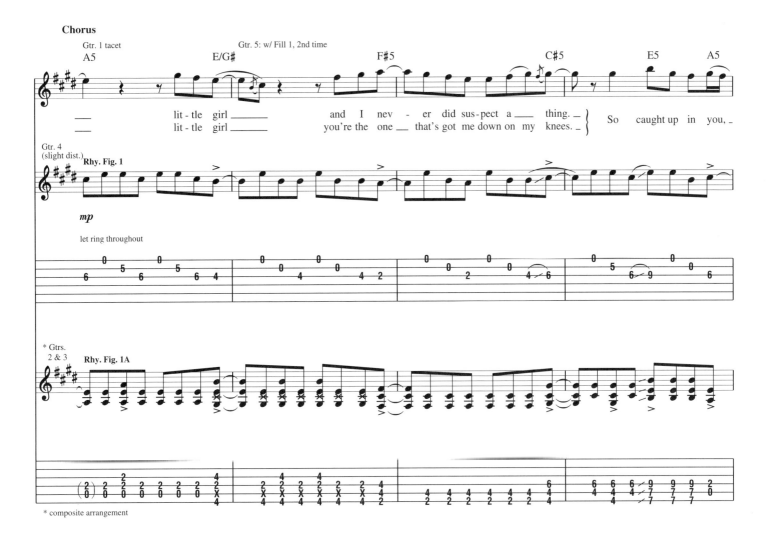

lit - tle girl ____ and I nev - er did sus-pect a __ thing. _
lit - tle girl ____ you're the one __ that's got me down on my knees. _ So caught up in you, _

* composite arrangement

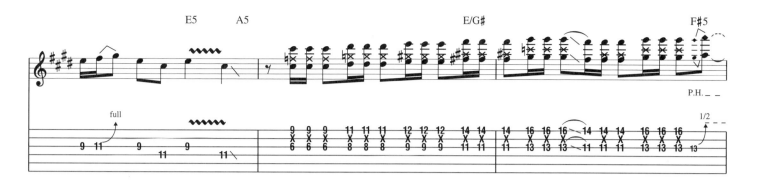

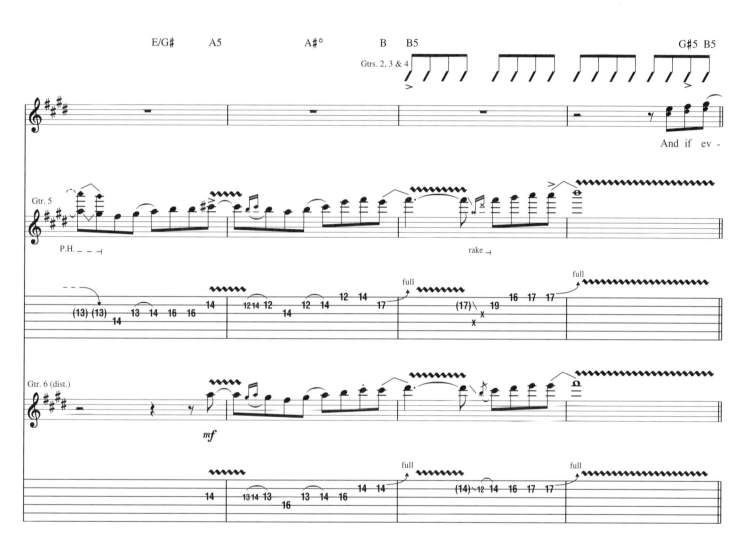

Interlude

Gtrs. 2, 3 & 4: w/ Rhy. Figs. 2 & 2A, simile
Gtrs. 5 & 6 tacet

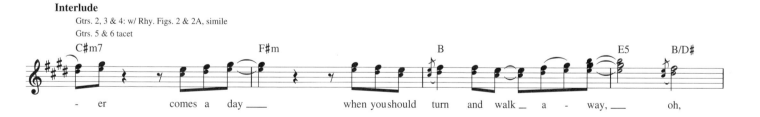

-er   comes a   day ____   when you should   turn   and   walk ___   a - way, ___   oh,

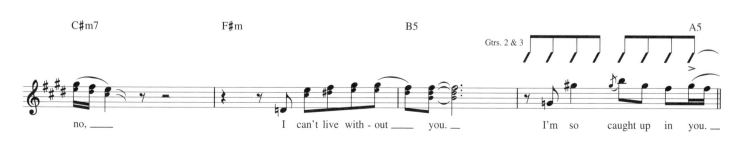

no, ____   I   can't   live   with - out ____   you. ___   I'm   so   caught   up   in   you. ___

11

you're the one _____ who caught _ me, an' taught _ me, an' got me so caught up in you._

Outro-Guitar Solo

Gtrs. 2, 3 & 4: w/ Rhy. Figs. 3 & 3A, simile, till fade

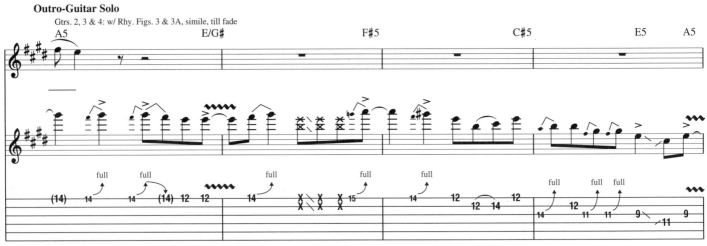

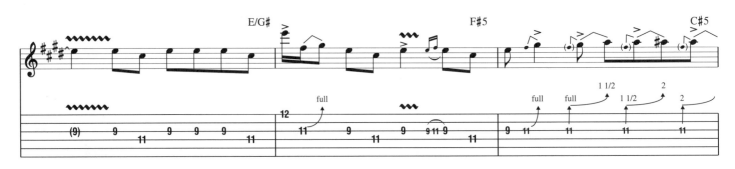

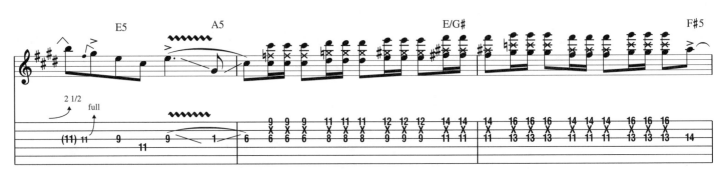

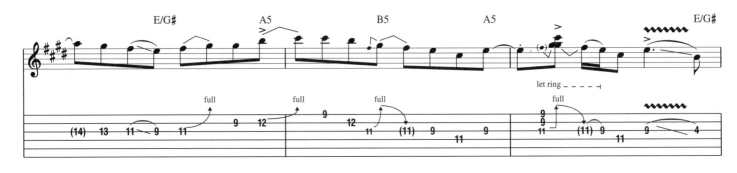

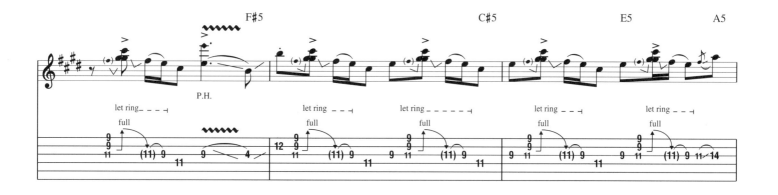

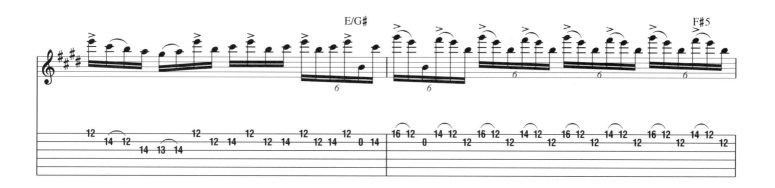

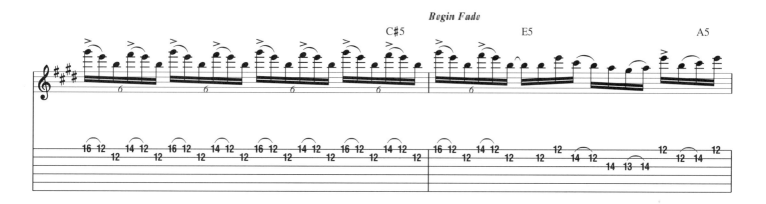

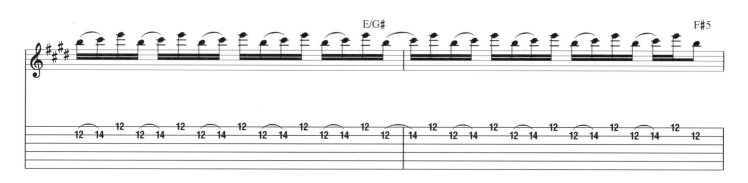

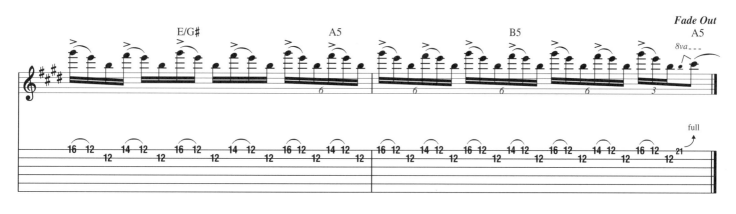

Down Boys

Words and Music by Jani Lane, Joey Allen, Jerry Dixon, Steven Sweet and Erik Turner

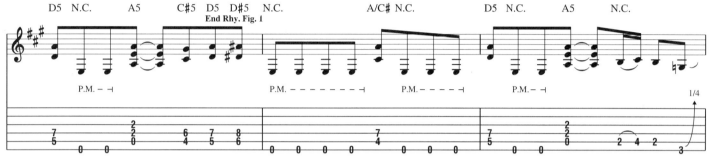

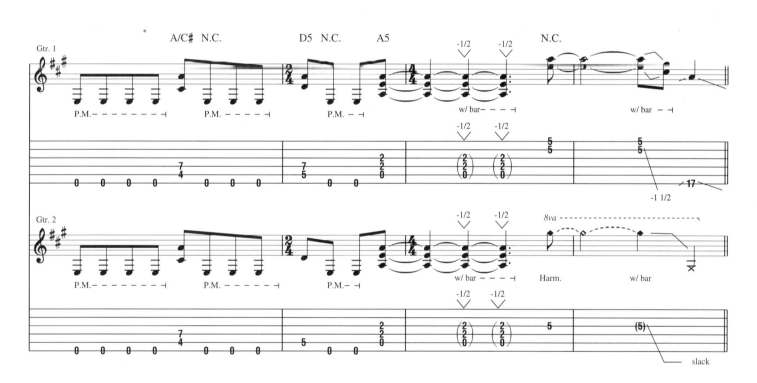

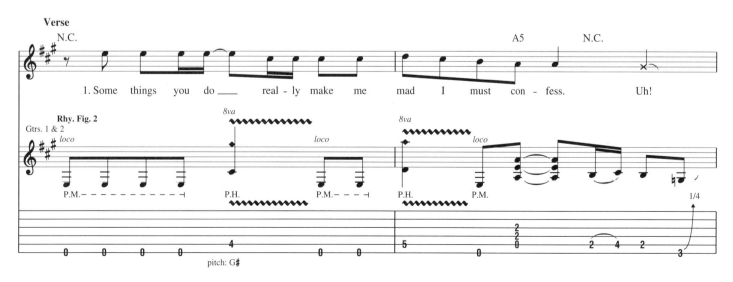

1. Some things you do ___ real-ly make me mad I must con-fess. Uh!

1st & 3rd times, Gtr. 3: w/ Riff A

E5   B5   A5   C#5   N.C.

know. __   Who knows __   One mil - lion miles an hour, __ head-ed out

giving me the run - a - round   make me feel like a fool.   Got a lot of nerve to call me cheap,

1st & 3rd times, Gtr. 3: w/ Riff A

A5   E5   B5   A5   C#5

to where the down boys __ go.   Now I don't care where we go tonight, take me a-long with you. __

even though it's true.

Pre-Chorus

To Coda ⊕

2nd time, Gtr. 1: w/ Fill 2

G5   Dsus4   D   C5

1., 3. Whoa.   Can we re - wind __ to where we've been?   Oh, I wish you'd take a look and

Gtrs. 1 & 2

Chorus

2nd time, Gtrs. 1 & 2: w/ Rhy. Fill 1

D5   E5   B5   A5   E5   B5   A5

see the shape __ I'm in. __ Where the down boys go, go!   Where the down boys go, go! __

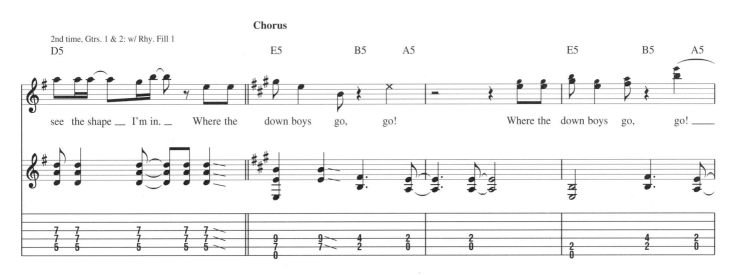

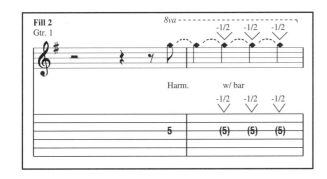

Fill 2
Gtr. 1

Rhy. Fill 1
Gtrs. 1 & 2

Additional Lyrics

3. Some things you do really make me made,
   I must confess.
   The way the streetlight silhouettes our things,
   Inside your dress.
   Oo, yeah.

867-5309/Jenny

Words and Music by Alex Call and James Keller

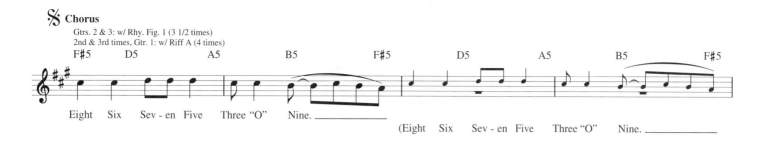

Interlude
Gtr. 1: w/ Riff A (4 times)
Gtrs. 2 & 3 tacet

good time, for a good time call. . . .

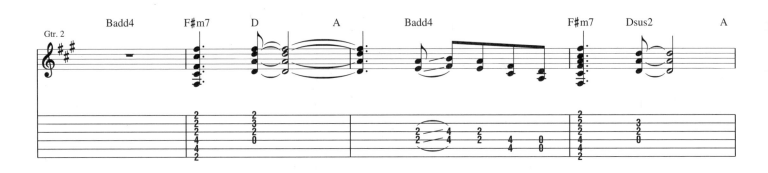

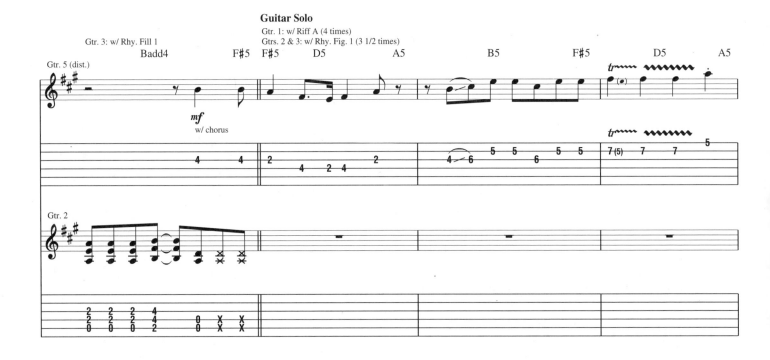

Guitar Solo
Gtr. 1: w/ Riff A (4 times)
Gtrs. 2 & 3: w/ Rhy. Fig. 1 (3 1/2 times)

Gtr. 3: w/ Rhy. Fill 1

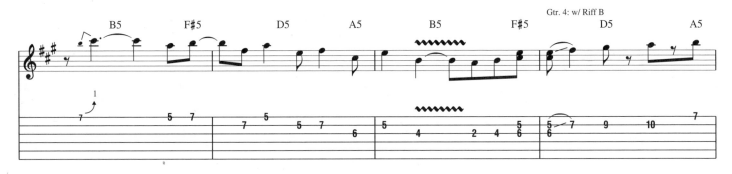

Gtr. 4: w/ Riff B

Every Breath You Take

Written and Composed by Sting

Eye of the Tiger

Theme from ROCKY III
Words and Music by Frank Sullivan and Jim Peterik

Verse

Gtr. 2 tacet
Gtr. 1: w/ Riff A, 2 times

1. Ris - in' up, back on the street,_ did my time,_ took my chanc - es.

Went the dis - tance, now I'm back on _ my feet, just a man and his will to sur - vive. _

𝄋 Verse

Gtr. 1: w/ Riff A, 2 times, 1st time
Gtr. 1 tacet, 2nd time

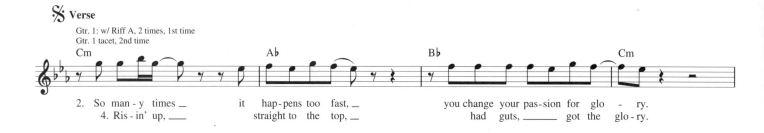

2. So man - y times _ it hap - pens too fast, _ you change your pas - sion for glo - ry.
4. Ris - in' up, ___ straight to the top, _ had guts, ____ got the glo - ry.

Gtr. 1: w/ Riff A, 2nd time

Don't lose your grip _ on the dreams of _ the past, you must fight just to keep them a - live. _
Went the dis - tance, now I'm not gon - na stop, just a man and his will to sur - vive. _ } It's the

Chorus

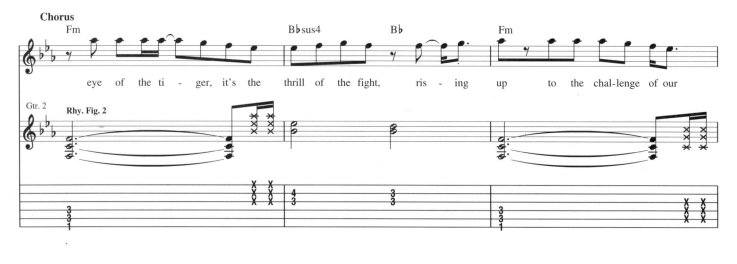

eye of the ti - ger, it's the thrill of the fight, ris - ing up to the chal - lenge of our

Gtr. 2
Rhy. Fig. 2

ri - val. And _ the last known sur - vi - vor stalks his prey in the night, and _ he's

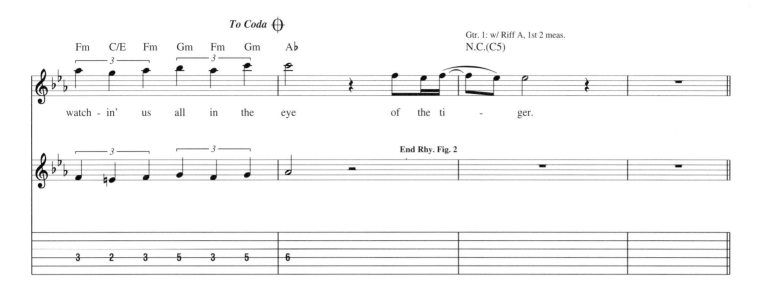

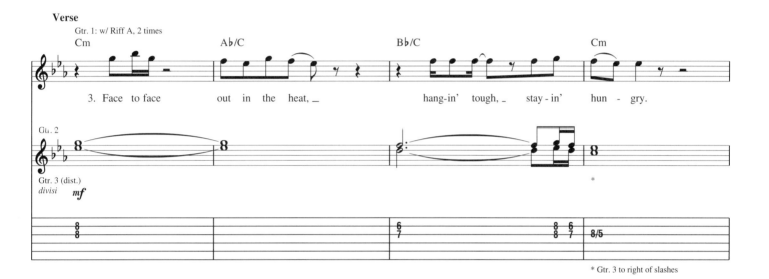

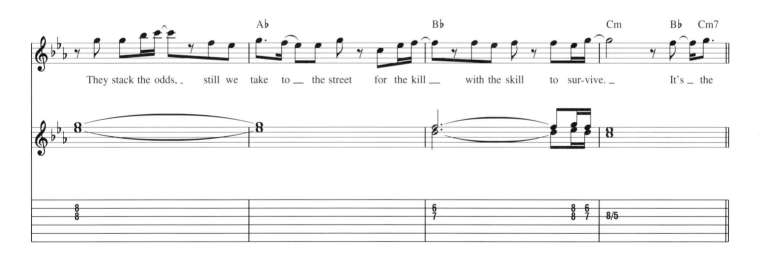

ri - val. And __ the last known sur - vi - vor stalks his prey in the night, and __ he's

watch- in' us all in the eye of the ti - ger.

⊕ *Coda*

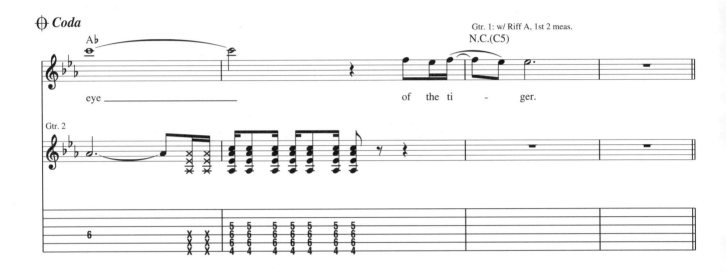

eye __ of the ti - ger.

Outro

The eye of the ti - ger.

The eye of the ti - ger. ___

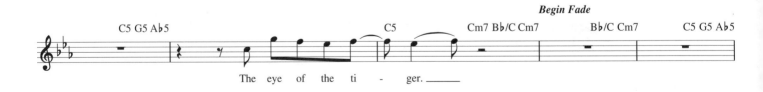

The eye of the ti - ger. ___

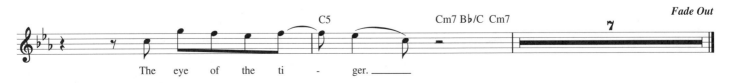

The eye of the ti - ger. ___

Fight for Your Right (To Party)

Words and Music by Rick Rubin, Adam Horovitz and Adam Yauch

Tune down 1/2 step:
(low to high) Eb–Ab–Db–Gb–Bb–Eb

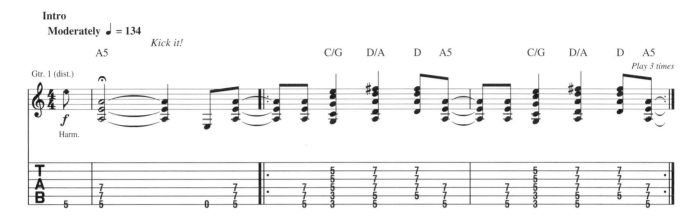

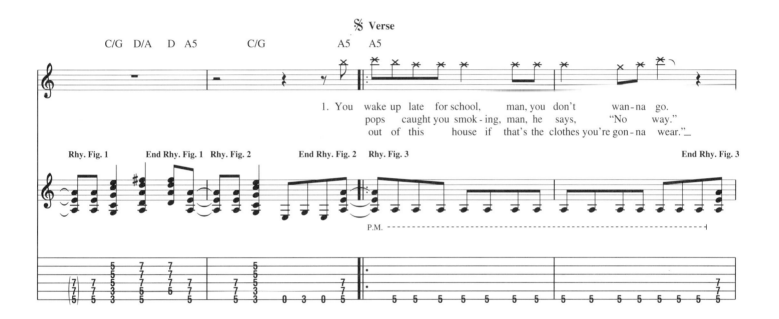

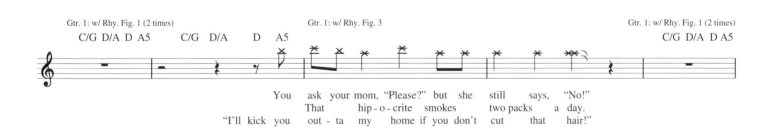

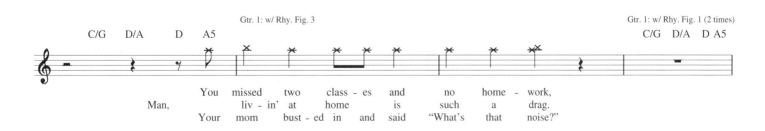

Heart and Soul

Words and Music by Mike Chapman and Nicky Chinn

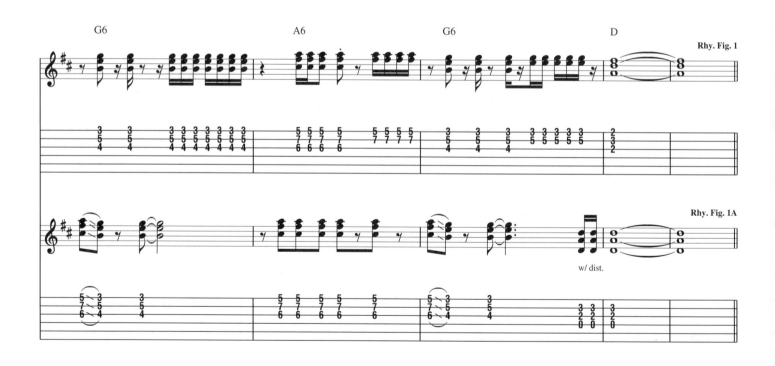

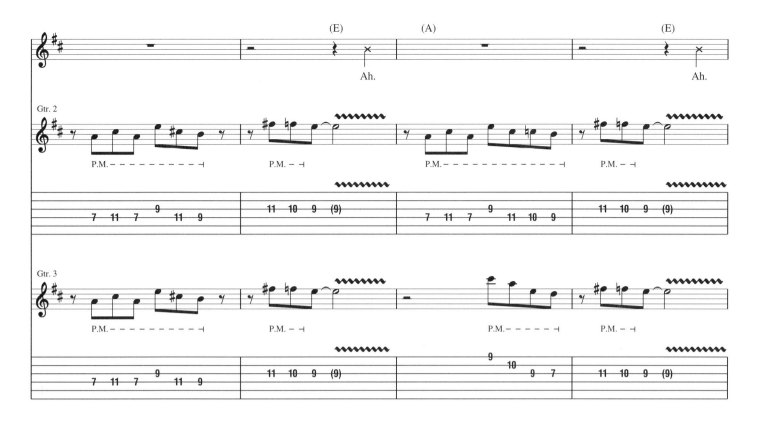

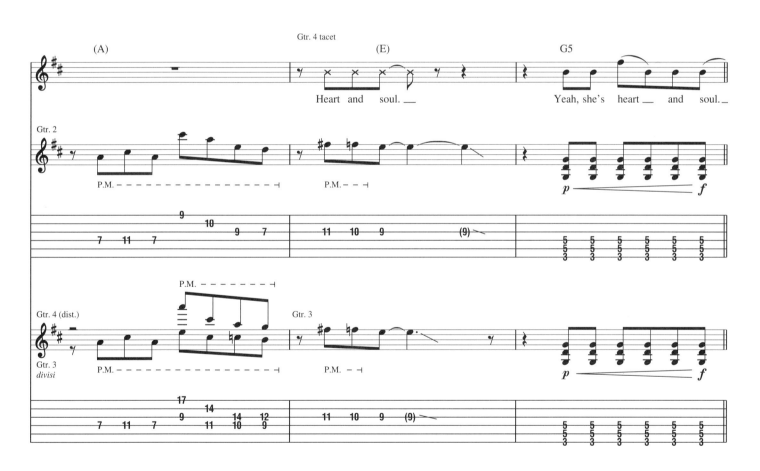

Chorus
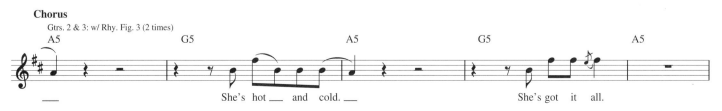

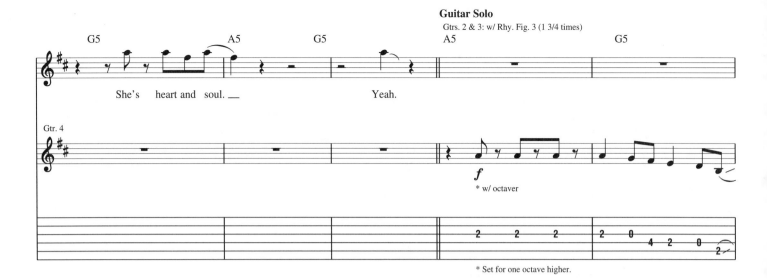

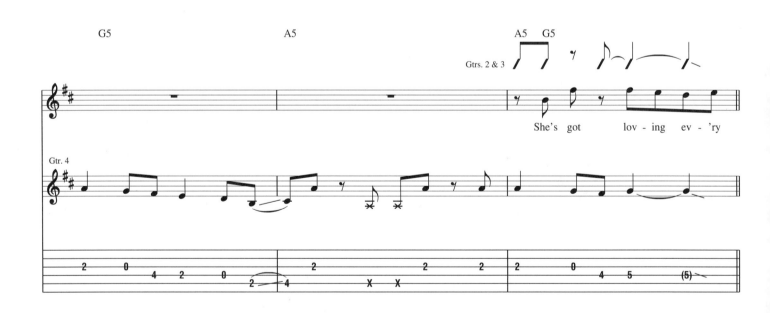

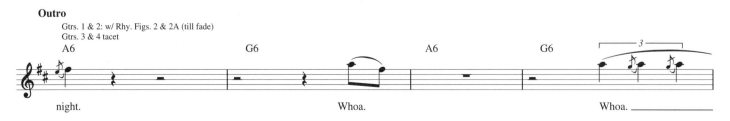

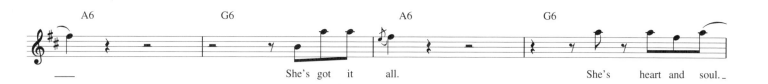

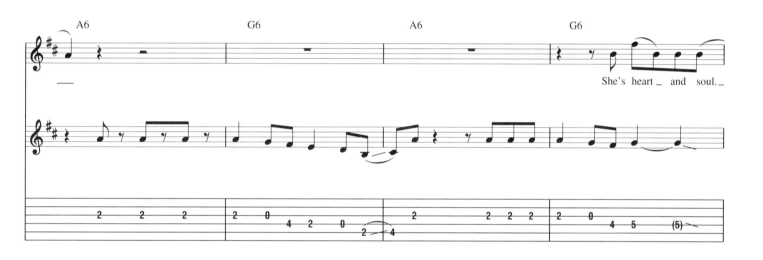

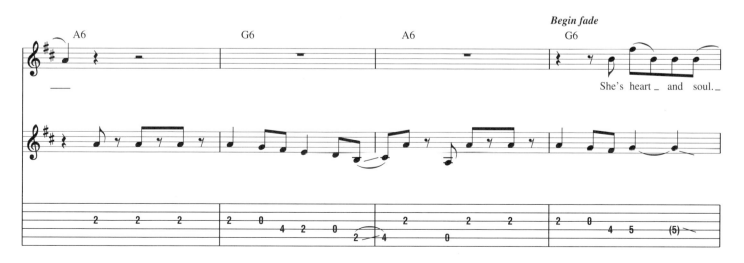

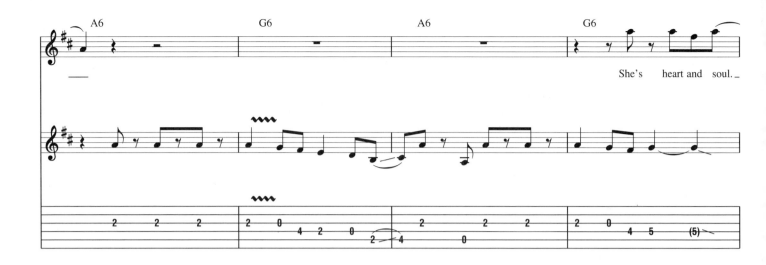

She's   heart and soul.

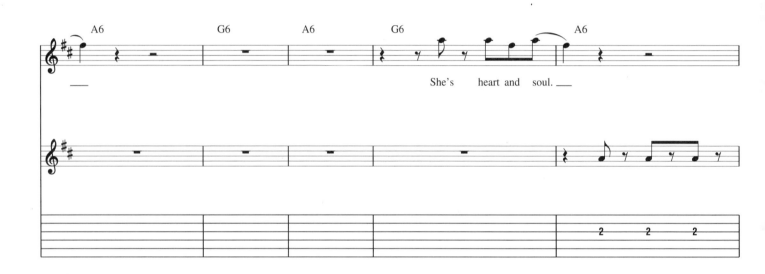

She's   heart and soul.

Additional Lyrics

3. Well, can't you see her standing there?
    See how she looks, see how she cares.
    I let her steal the night away from me.

4. Nine o'clock this morning
    She left without a warning.
    I let her take advantage of me.

Hit Me With Your Best Shot

Words and Music by Eddie Schwartz

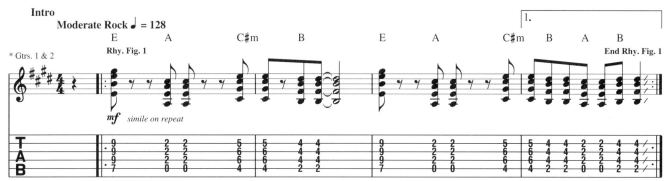

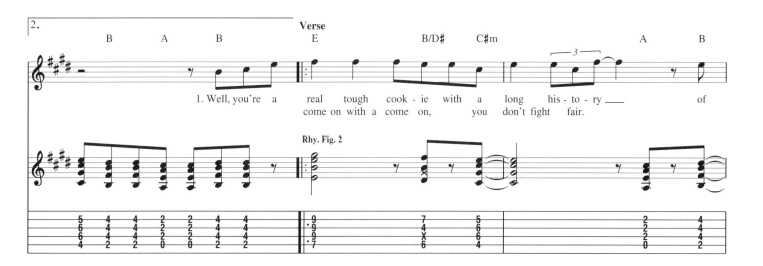

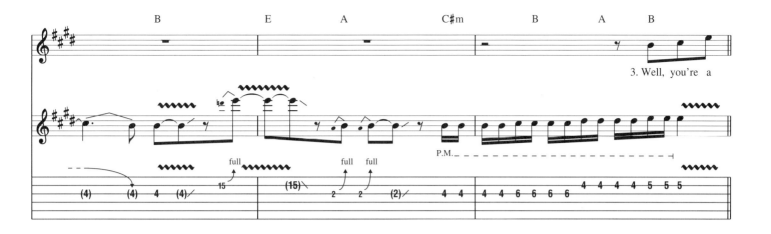

3. Well, you're a

Verse

real tough cook-ie with a long his-to-ry of break-ing lit-tle hearts like the one in me. Be-fore I

* Chord symbols reflect implied tonality.

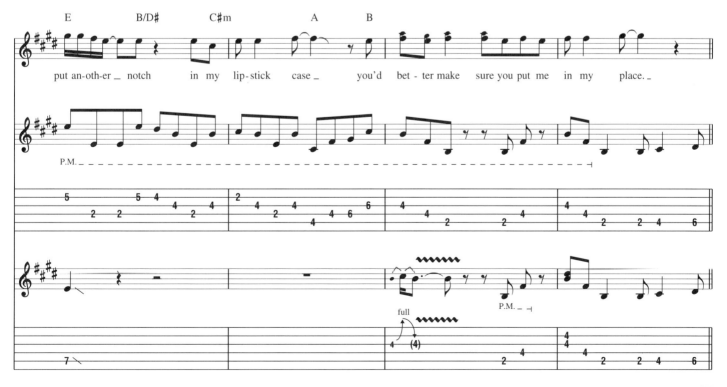

put an-oth-er _ notch in my lip-stick case _ you'd bet-ter make sure you put me in my place. _

I Love Rock 'N Roll

Words and Music by Alan Merrill and Jake Hooker

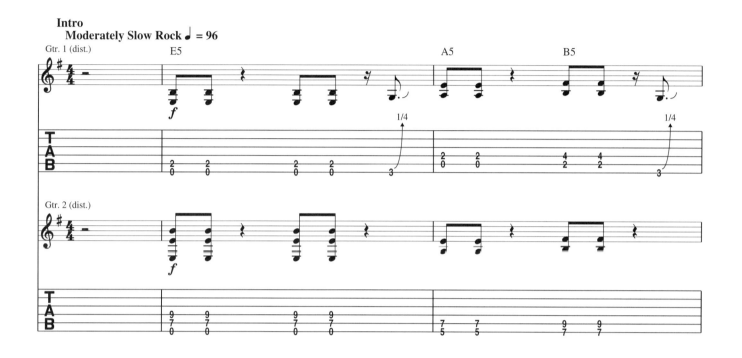

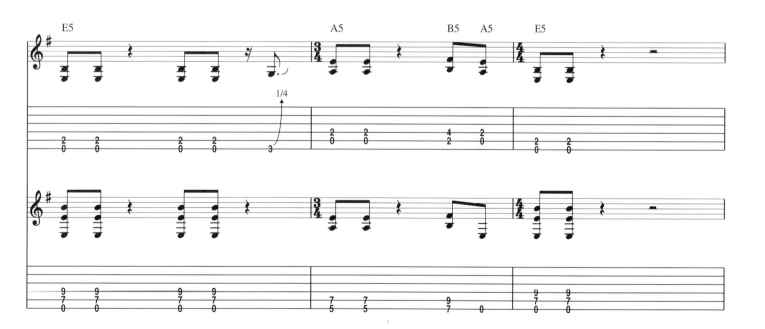

Verse

1. I saw him danc-in' there, __ by the re-cord ma-chine. I
smiled, so I got up __ and asked for his name.

simile on repeat

knew he must have been __ a-bout sev-en-teen. The beat was go-in' strong, __
"That don't mat-ter," he said, __ "'cause it's all the same." I said, "Can I take ya home __ where

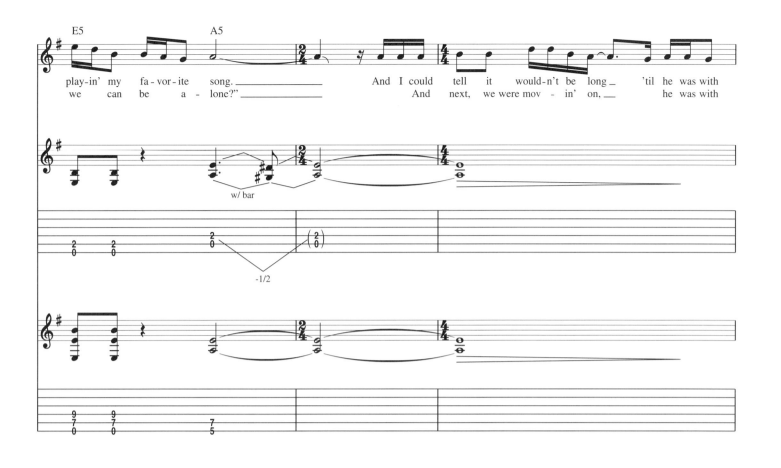

Chorus

lone?" _____ Next, we were mov - in' on, __ he was with me, yeah, me! And we'll be

Gtrs. 1 & 3 tacet

Gtr. 2 tacet
N.C.

Chorus

N.C.

mov - in' on, __ and sing-in' that same old song, yeah, with me, __ sing-in', I love rock 'n' roll, __ so

put an-oth-er dime in the juke-box, ba - by. I love rock 'n' roll, __ so come and take your time and dance with me.

54

In and Out of Love

Words and Music by Jon Bon Jovi

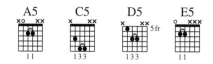

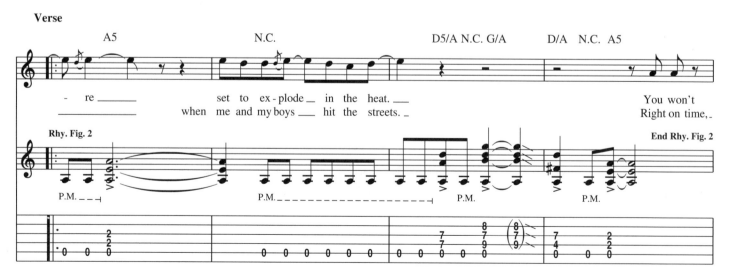

Gtr. 1: w/ Rhy. Fig. 2

N.C.   A5   N.C.   D5/A N.C. G/A   D/A N.C. A5

ti - re _____ 'cause ba - by was born _ with a beat. _____   Take you high -
_____ she's here to make my ___ life com- plete. _____   Then I'm long_

Pre-Chorus

N.C.   D5/G   N.C.   D5   Dsus4   D   N.C.

- er than you've ev- er known, _____ then drive you down ___ to drink-in' beers._   One
- gone, _ I got a - noth- er show. One more time, _ one mile _____ to go. _   One

Gtr. 1

w/ bar   P.M.

D5/G   N.C. D5/G N.C. D5/G N.C. D5/G N.C.   D5/G   N.C. D5   N.C. D5 N.C.   A5

I pick you up when you've had e - nough. _____   You've been burned,_ ba- by, les- son's learned. _____ In -
end- less night _ of fan- ta- sy. _   It's all she left ___ of her with me. _____

P.M.   P.M.   P.M.   P.M.   P.M.   P.M.

% Chorus

N.C. Am7 N.C. A5 N.C.   A5   N.C. Am7 N.C. A5   N.C.   A5

___ and out of love.   1., 2. Hear what I'm say - ing. _ In ___ and out of love. It's the way ___ that we're play - ing.   In _
                       3.   In ___ and out of love.   In _

Rhy. Fig. 3

Bridge

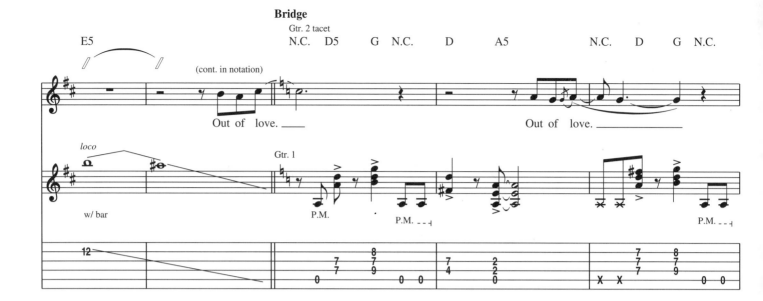

Out of love. _____

Out of love. _____

Out of love. _____

Out of love. _

In _

Breakdown

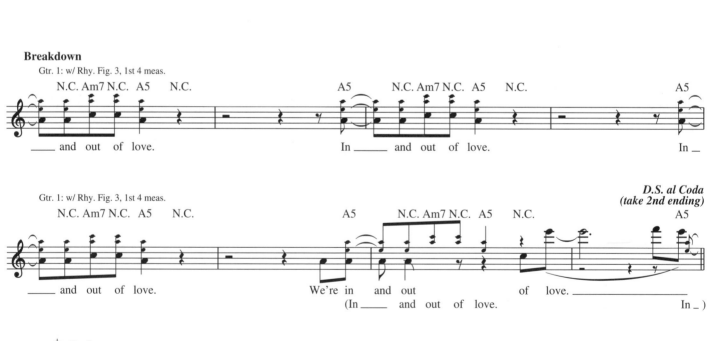

_____ and out of love.

In _____ and out of love.

In

_____ and out of love.

We're in and out of love. _____

(In _____ and out of love.

In _)

⊕ Coda

_____ and out of love.

In _ and out of love.

In _ and out of love.

In

Spoken: Hey, just how old are you anyway?

La Bamba

By Ritchie Valens

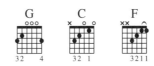

gra - cia, pa'ra mi pa'ra ti ___ y ar - ri - ba, ar - ri - ba.

Y ar - ri - ba, ar - ri - ba, por ti se - re, ___ por ti se - re, ___

Verse

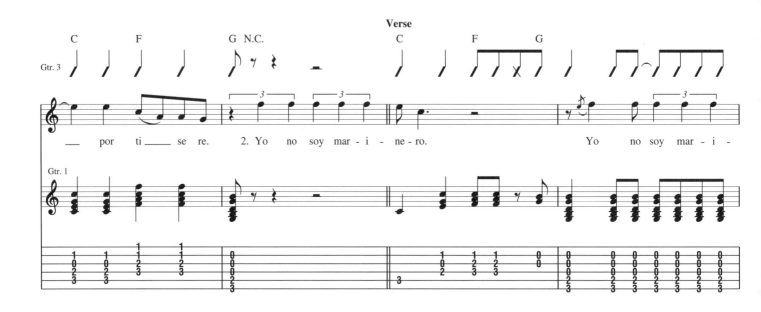

Gtr. 3

___ por ti ___ se - re. 2. Yo no soy mar - i - ne - ro. Yo no soy mar - i -

Gtr. 1

Gtrs. 1 & 3: w/ Rhy. Figs. 1 & 1A (2 times)

ne - ro, soy cap - i - tan, ___ soy cap - i - tan, ___ soy cap - i - tan. ___

Chorus

Gtr. 2: w/ Riff B (1 1/2 times)

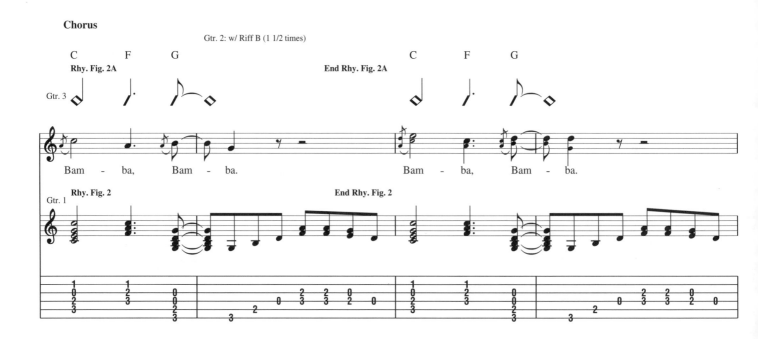

Rhy. Fig. 2A   End Rhy. Fig. 2A

Gtr. 3

Bam - ba, Bam - ba.   Bam - ba, Bam - ba.

Rhy. Fig. 2   End Rhy. Fig. 2

Gtr. 1

*Nylon str. (Mexican Folk instruments are used for this section, arr. here for standard gtrs.)

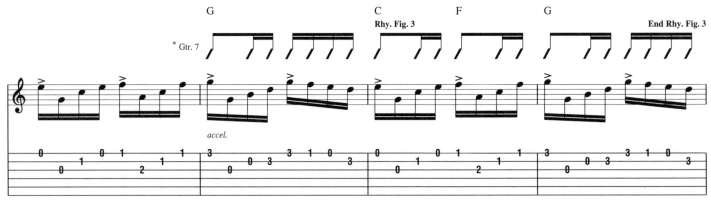

*Nylon str. (Mexican Folk instruments are used for this section, arr. here for standard gtrs.)

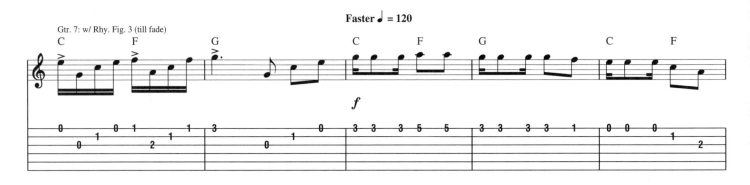

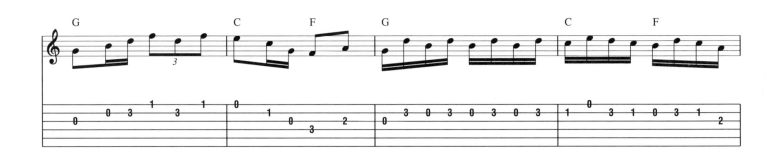

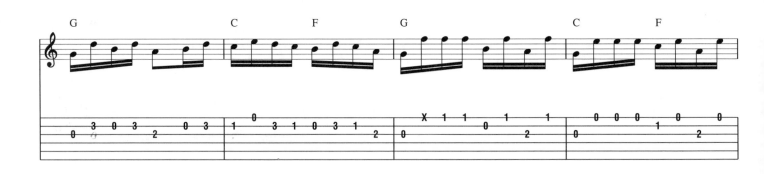

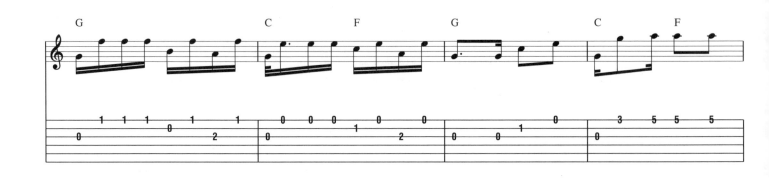

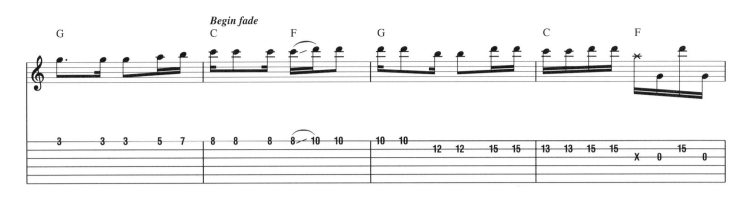

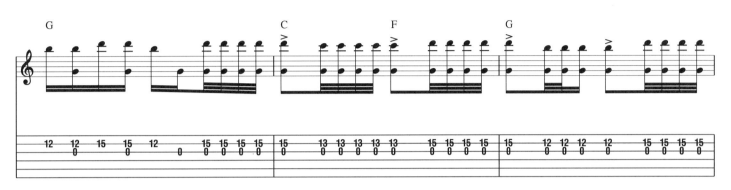

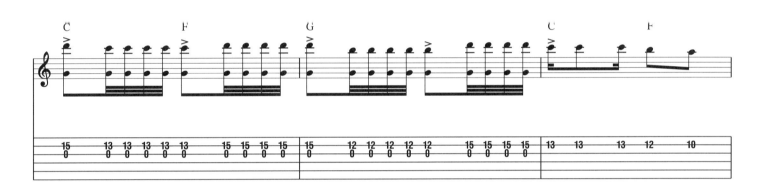

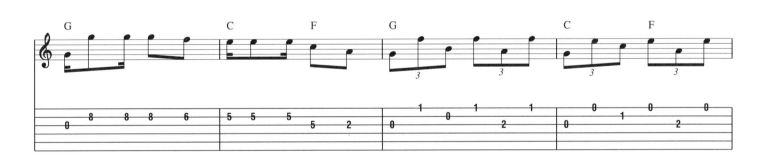

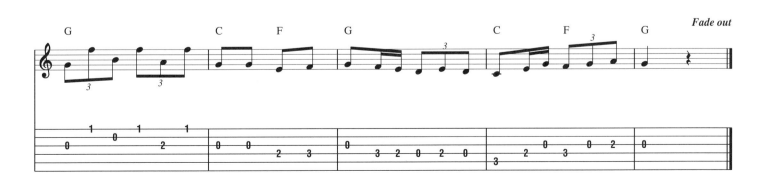

Land of Confusion

Words and Music by Tony Banks, Phil Collins and Mike Rutherford

Gtr. 1: w/ Rhy. Fig. 2 (3 times)

E5　C5　D5　B5　E5　C5

and these are ___ the hands we're giv - en　Oh. _____ Use them ___ and

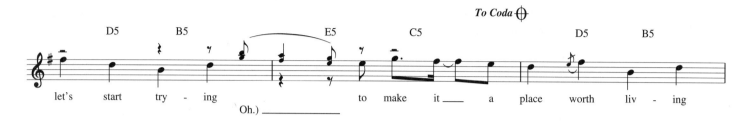

To Coda ⊕

D5　B5　E5　C5　D5　B5

let's start try - ing　　Oh.) _____ to make it ___ a place worth liv - ing

Gtr. 1: w/ Riff A

A　　Am　　D5/E

1.　　2.

in.

Bridge

C#m　　F#/C#

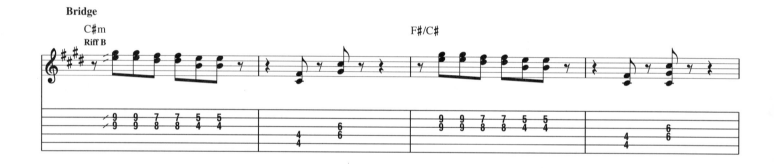

Riff B

A/C#　　　　E　E/D#　C#m　F#

I re-mem - ber ___ long a-

End Riff B

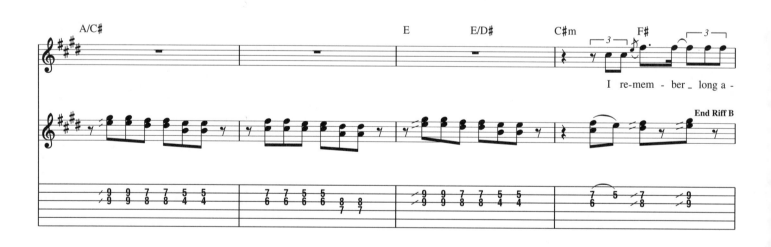

Gtr. 1: w/ Riff B

C#m　　F#/C#

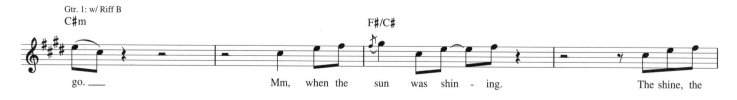

go. ___　Mm, when the sun was shin - ing.　The shine, the

stars were bright __ all through __ the night. __ And the sound of __ your laugh - ter

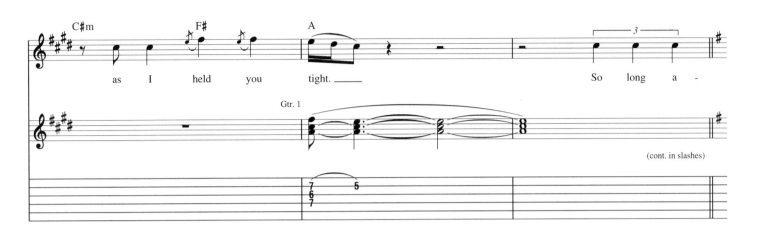

as I held you tight. ____ So long a -

Gtr. 1

(cont. in slashes)

Interlude

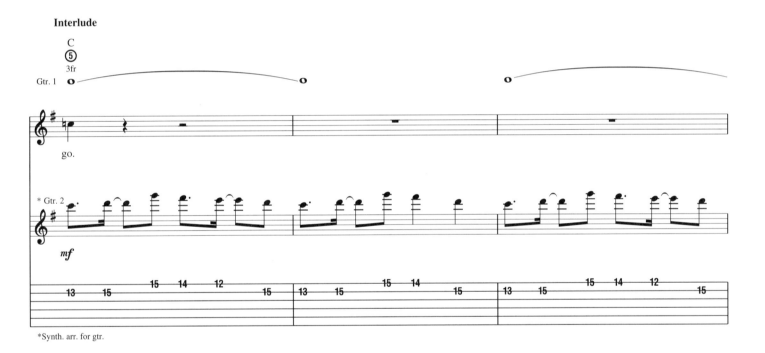

go.

* Gtr. 2

*Synth. arr. for gtr.

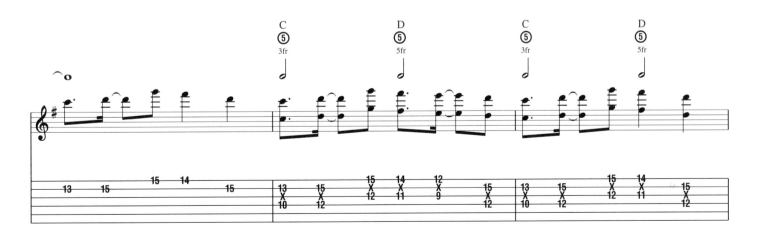

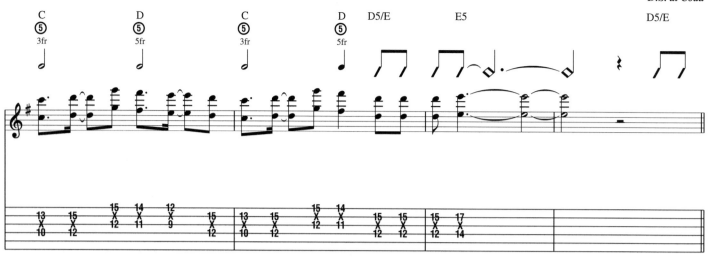

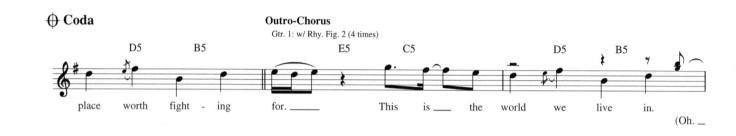

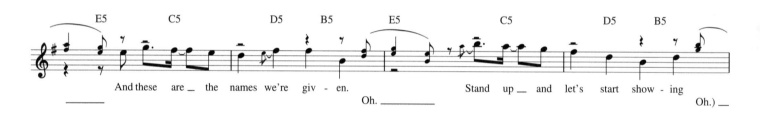

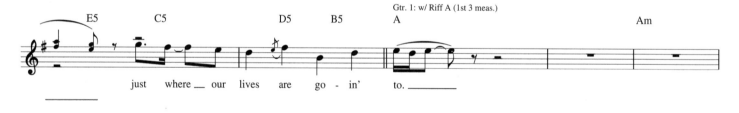

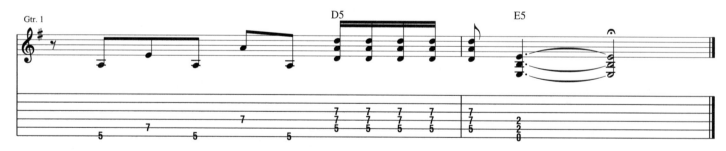

Additional Lyrics

4. I won't be coming home tonight.
My generation will put it right.
We're not just making promises,
That we know we'll never keep.

Love Struck Baby

Written by Stevie Ray Vaughan

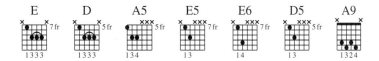

Intro

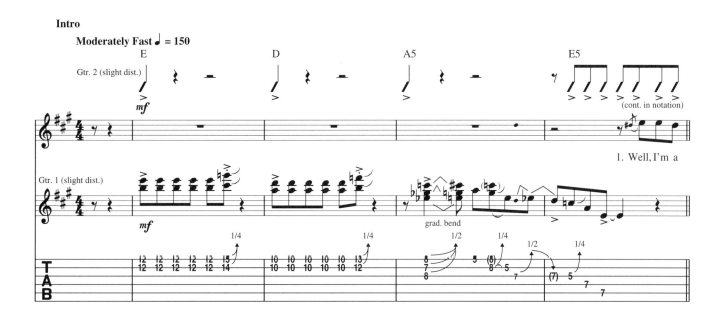

1. Well, I'm a

Verse

love struck ba - by, I ___ must con - fess. ___ Life ___ with - out ya, dar - lin' is a

* Chord symbols reflect overall tonality.

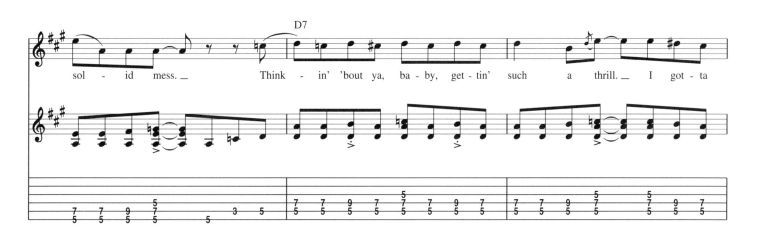

sol - id mess. ___ Think - in' 'bout ya, ba - by, get - tin' such a thrill. ___ I got - ta

have you ba - by, can't __ get my fill. __ I __ love you, ba - by, an' I

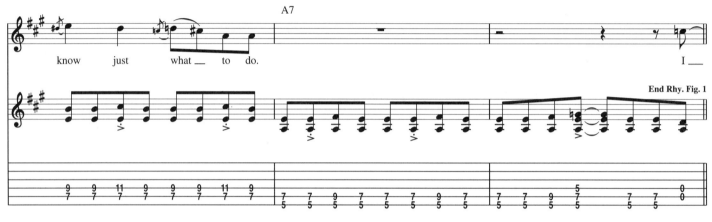

know just what __ to do.

End Rhy. Fig. 1

I __

𝄋 **Pre-Chorus**

__ still __ re - mem - ber, let it be said, __ the way __ ya make me feel, __ it takes a
- 'ry time __ I see ya make me feel so fine, __ my heart __ beat - in' cra - zy,
__ start - ed fly - in' ev - 'ry time we meet. __ Don't - cha know, ba - by, ya knock

simile on repeats

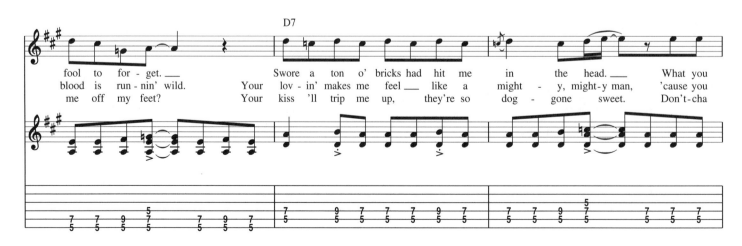

fool to for - get. __ Swore a ton o' bricks had hit me in the head. __ What you
blood is run - nin' wild. Your lov - in' makes me feel __ like a might - y, might - y man, 'cause you
me off my feet? Your kiss 'll trip me up, they're so dog - gone sweet. Don't - cha

Guitar Solo

Gtr. 2: w/ Rhy. Fig. 1, 3 times, simile

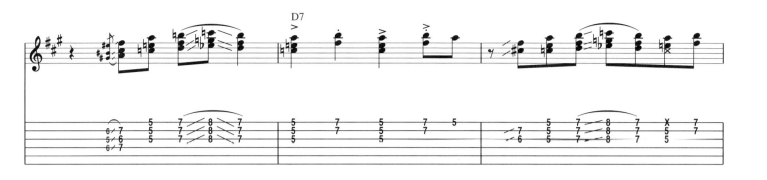

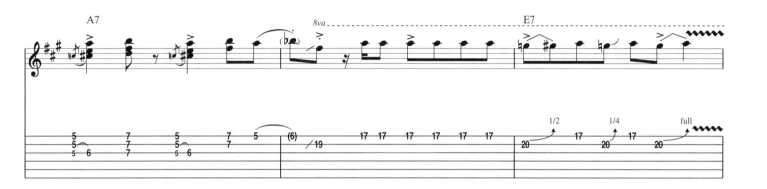

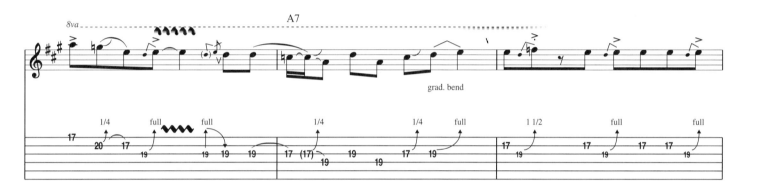

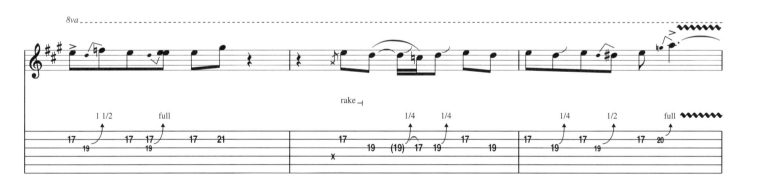

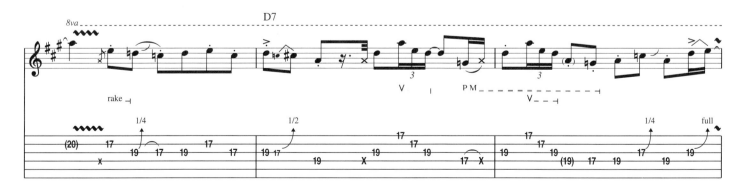

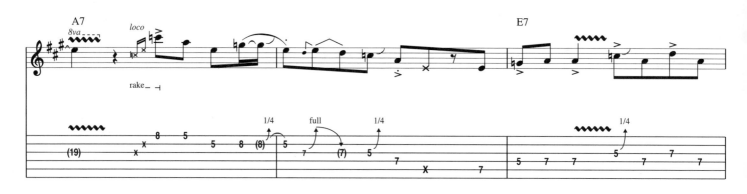

D.S. al Coda

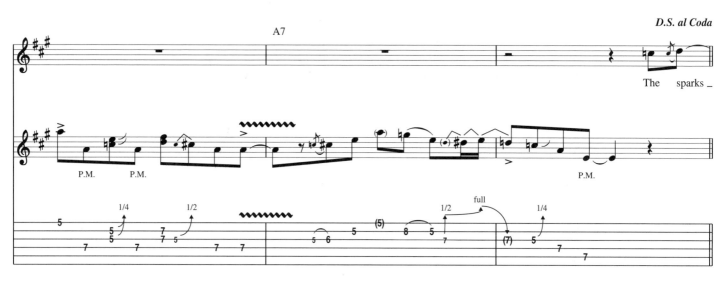

The sparks

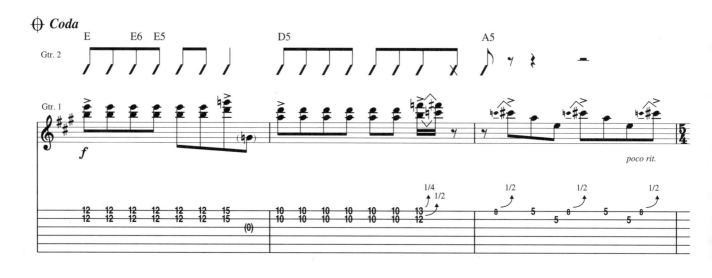

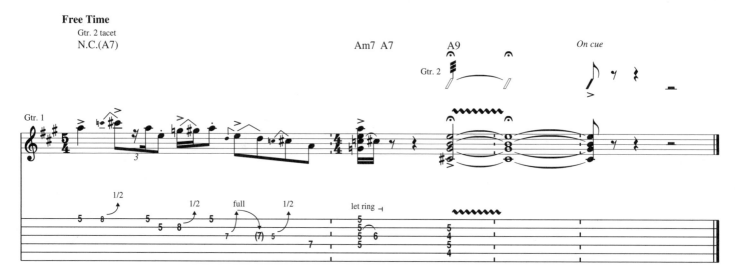

(Bang Your Head) Metal Health

Words and Music by Carlos Cavazo, Kevin Dubrow, Frankie Banali and Tony Cavazo

Verse

Gtr. 1 tacet

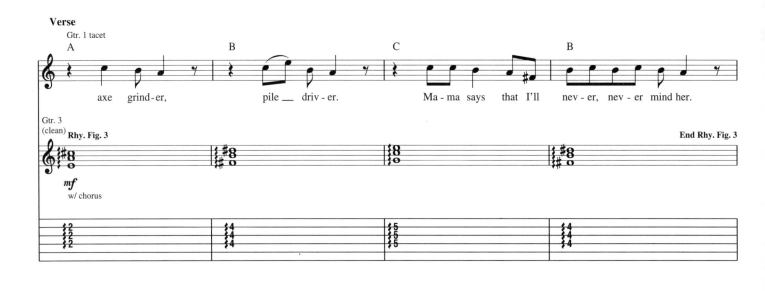

axe grind-er, pile __ driv-er. Ma-ma says that I'll nev-er, nev-er mind her.

Got no brains, __ I'm in - sane. __ The teach-er says that I'm

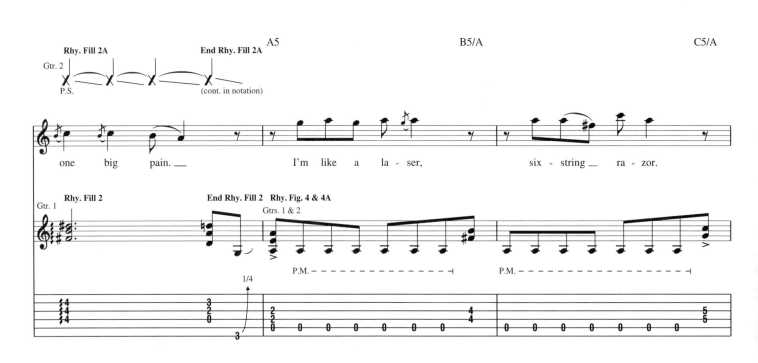

one big pain. __ I'm like a la-ser, six - string __ ra - zor.

I got a mouth like an al - li - ga-tor. I want it loud-er,

and I'm a keep-er.   I'm not a los-er and I ain't no weep-er.   I got the boys

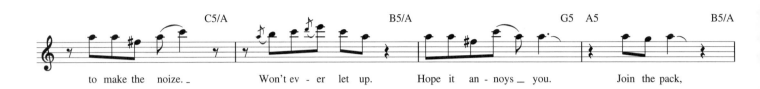

to make the noize. _   Won't ev - er let up.   Hope it an - noys _ you.   Join the pack,

Chorus

fill the crack.   Well, now you're here, _ there's no way back. _____   Bang your head!

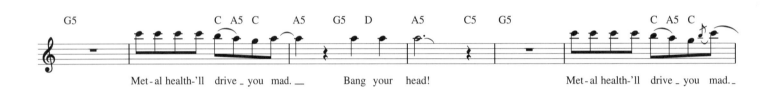

Met - al health-'ll drive _ you mad. _   Bang your head!   Met - al health-'ll drive _ you mad. _

Bridge

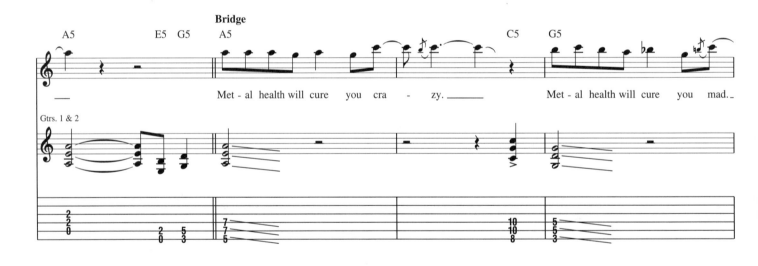

_   Met - al health will cure you cra - zy. _____   Met - al health will cure you mad. _

_   Met - al health is what we all _____ need. _   It's what we ought - a have. _

Guitar Solo

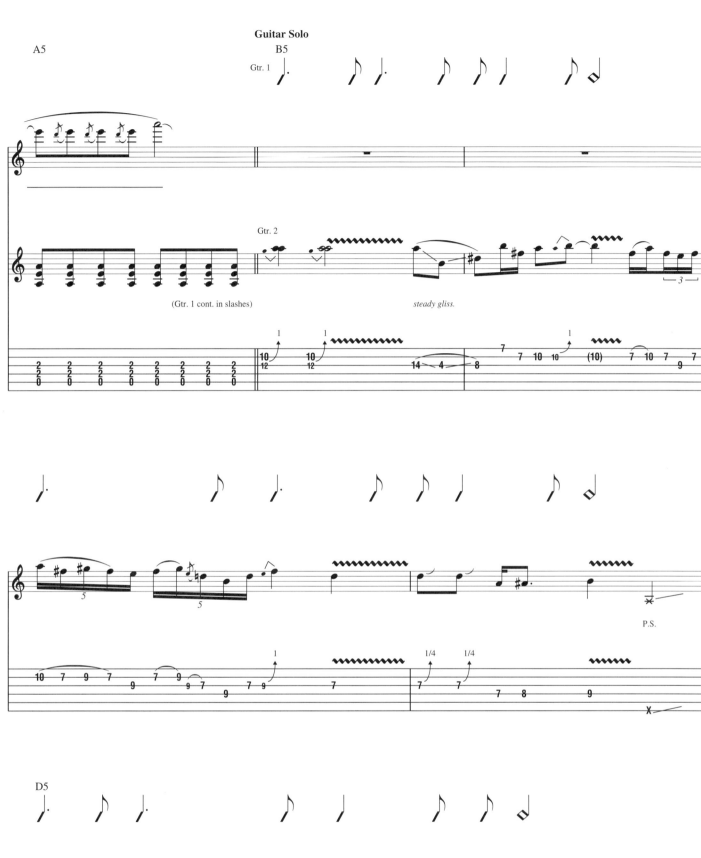

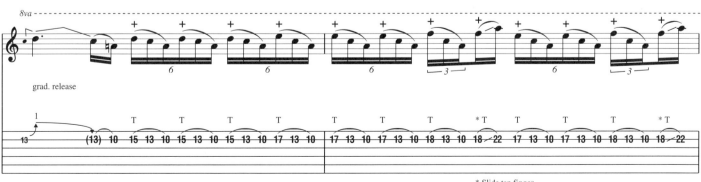

* Slide tap finger

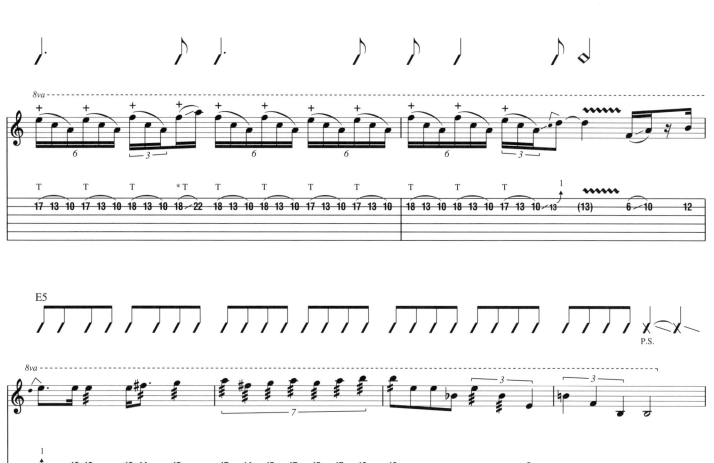

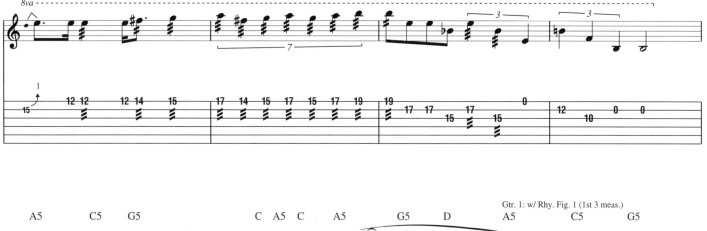

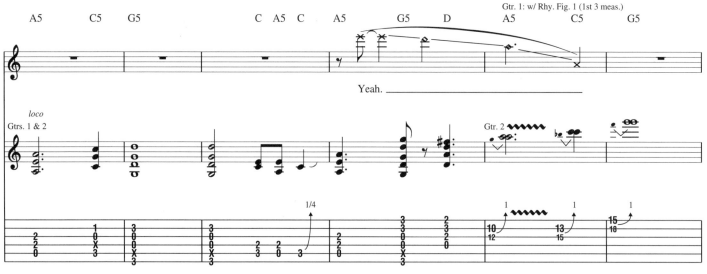

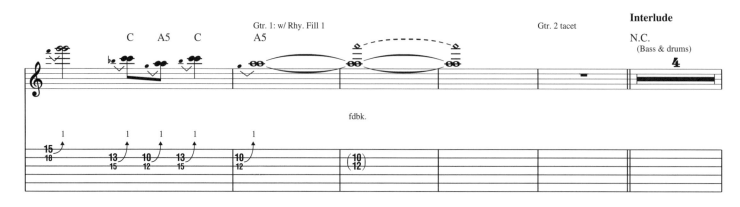

The bad boys are gon-na ___ set you right. Oh, rock on, rock ya, rock ya.

Outro-Guitar Solo

Gtrs. 1 & 2: w/ Rhy. Fig. 1 (1 3/4 times)

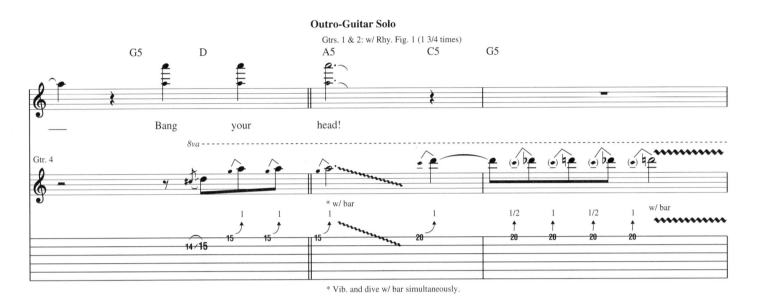

Bang your head!

* Vib. and dive w/ bar simultaneously.

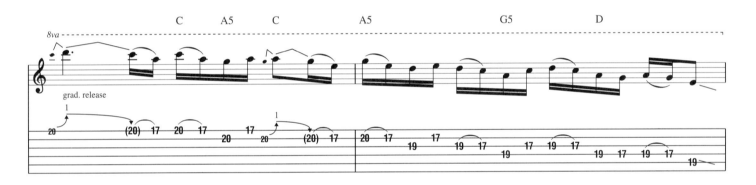

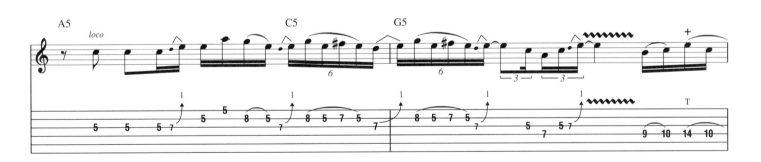

Free time

Gtr. 4: w/ misc. pick scrapes, till end

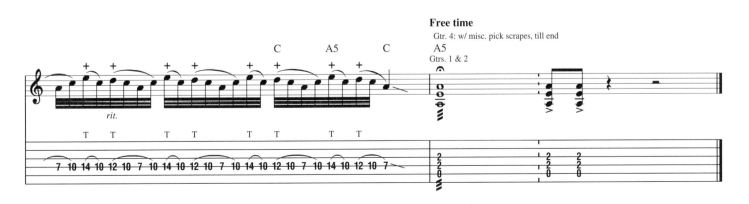

Money for Nothing

Words and Music by Mark Knopfler and Sting

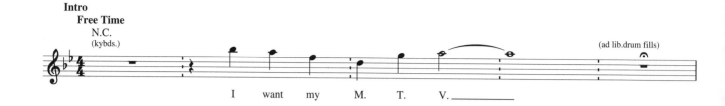

I want my M. T. V.

* Chord symbols reflect implied tonality.

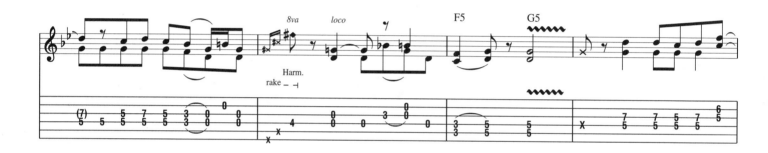

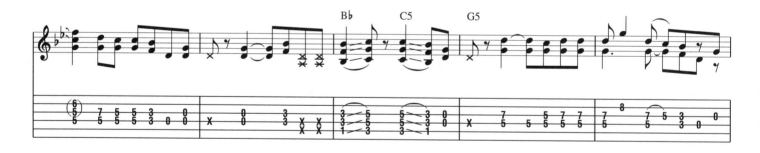

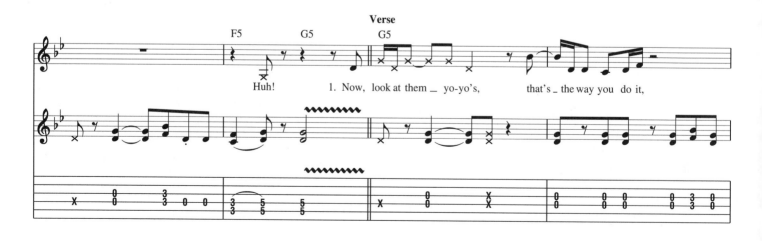

pitch : D

Outro

Lis-ten here. Now, that ain't work-ing, that's the way you do it, you play the gui - tar on the M. T. V.

That ain't _ work - in, that's _

_ the way you do it, mon-ey for noth-in' and your chicks for free. _ Mon-ey for noth-in',

and your chicks for free. _ Get your mon-ey for noth - in'

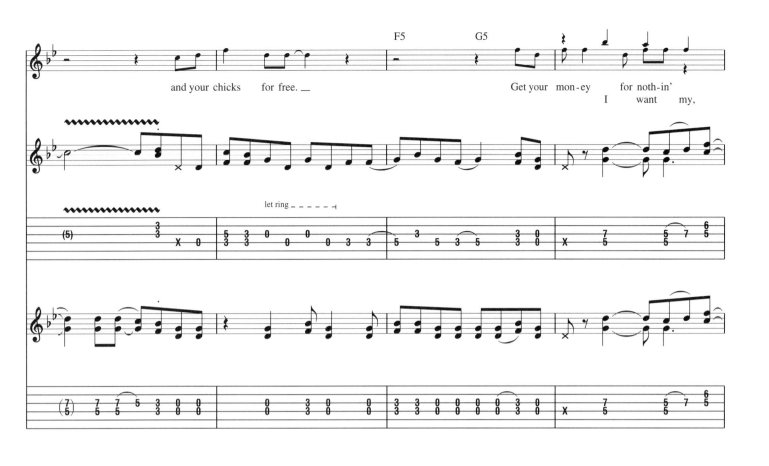

and your chicks for free. __

F5　　　　G5

Get your mon-ey for noth-in'
I want my,

let ring _ _ _ _ _ ⌐

Begin Fade

Bb5　　　　C5

and your chicks for free. __
I want my,
I want my M. T. __ V.

Get your

*Gtrs. 1 & 2

* composite arrangement

Fade Out

G5

Bb5　　　　C5

mon-ey for noth-in'
I want my,
I want my,
and your chicks for free. __
I want my M. T. __ V.

Mony, Mony

Words and Music by Bobby Bloom, Tommy James, Ritchie Cordell and Bo Gentry

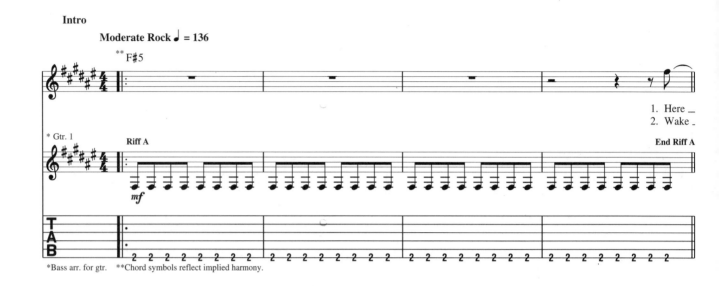

*Bass arr. for gtr.   **Chord symbols reflect implied harmony.

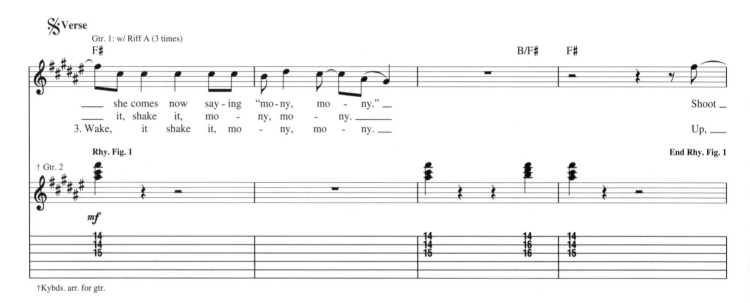

†Kybds. arr. for gtr.

Interlude

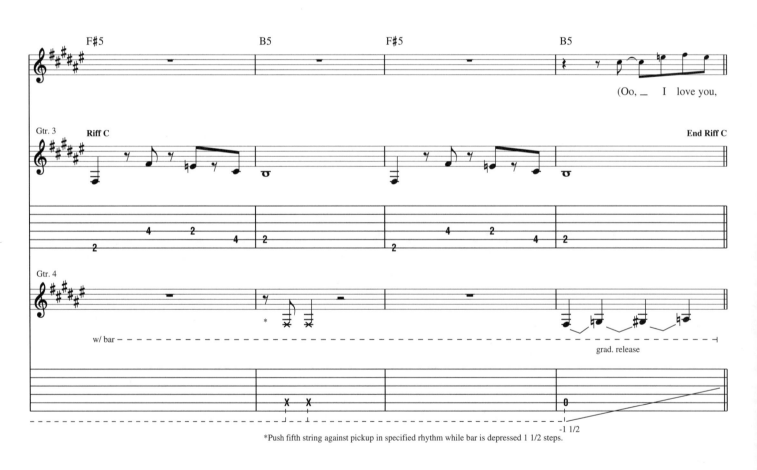

*Push fifth string against pickup in specified rhythm while bar is depressed 1 1/2 steps.

Bridge

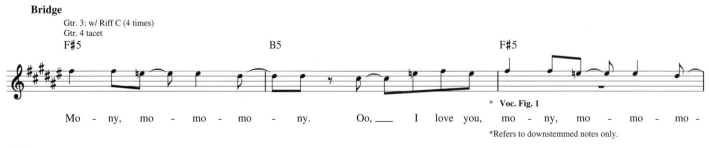

*Refers to downstemmed notes only.

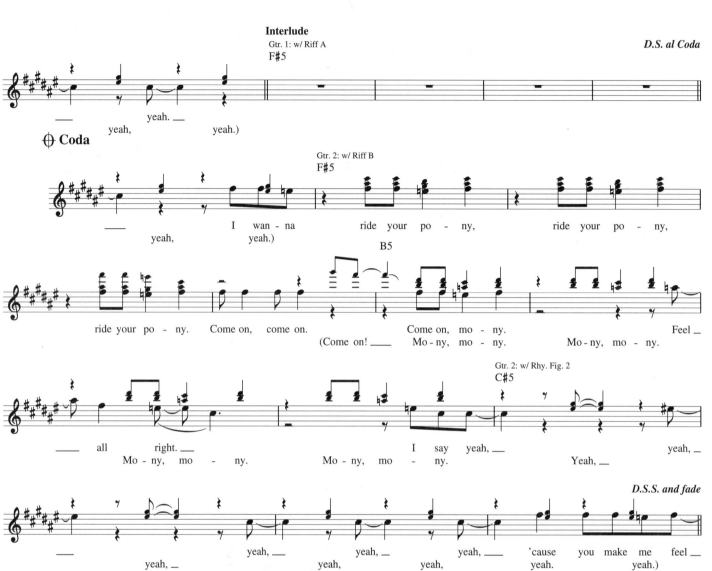

Additional Lyrics

2nd Chorus:
Cause you make me feel
So good, so good. Well, I feel all right.
You so fine, you so fine, you so fine.
I will be all right.
I say yeah....

3rd Chorus:
Cause you make me feel
So good, so good, so good.
Feel all right, all right, so fine.
Well, I feel all right.
I say yeah....

4th Chorus:
Cause you make me feel
So good, so good, so good.
Come on! Yeah, all right.
Well, I feel so good.
I say yeah....

Rag Doll

Words and Music by Steven Tyler, Joe Perry, Holly Knight and Jim Vallance

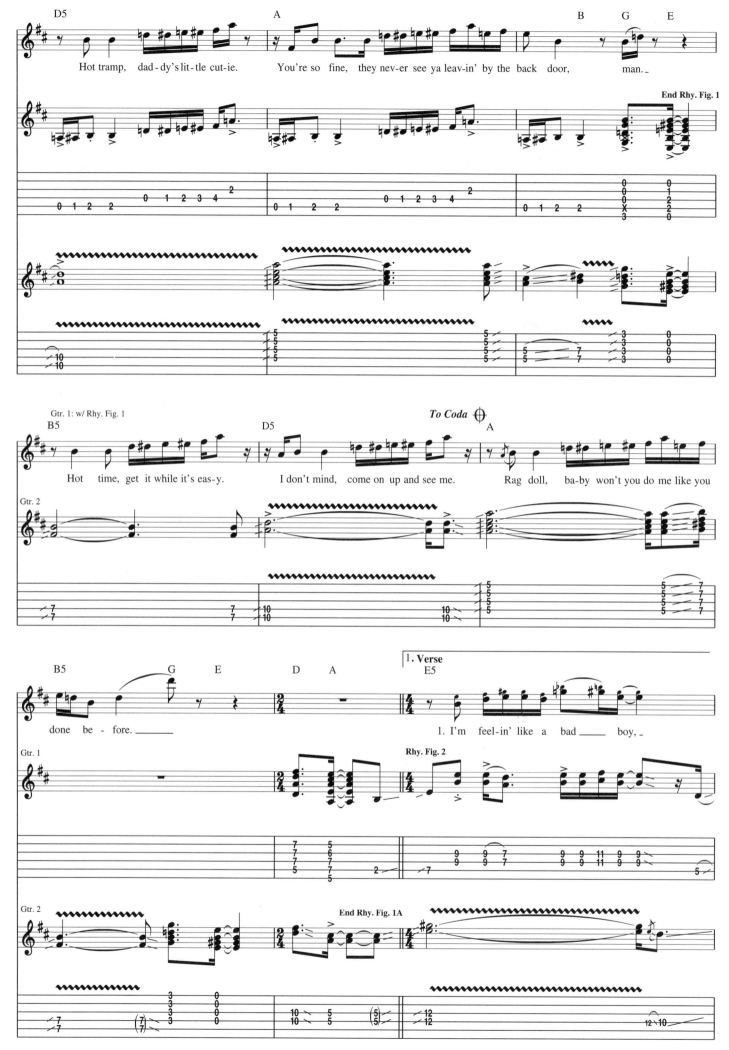

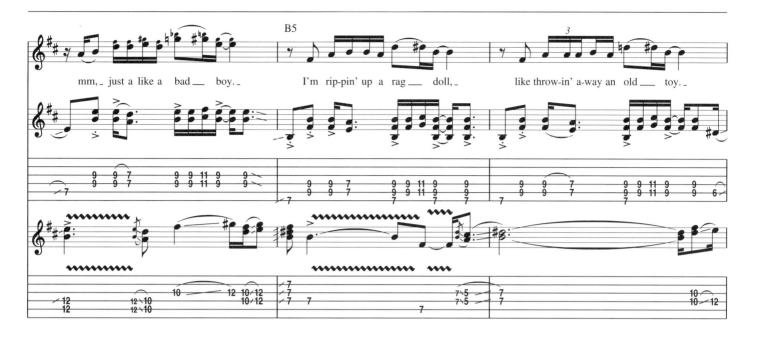

mm, __ just a like a bad __ boy. __   I'm rip-pin' up a rag __ doll, __   like throw-in' a-way an old __ toy. __

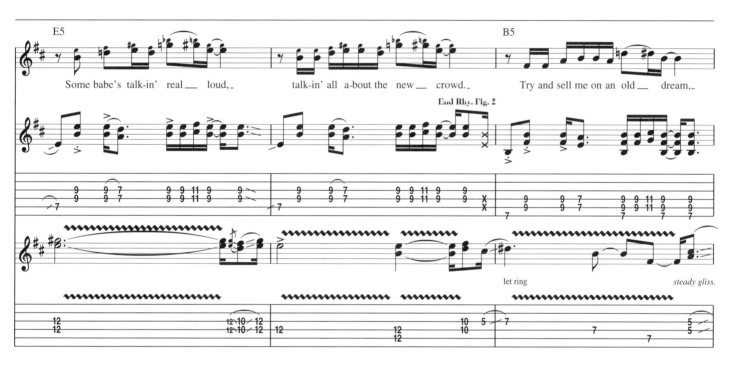

Some babe's talk-in' real __ loud, __   talk-in' all a-bout the new __ crowd. __   Try and sell me on an old __ dream, __

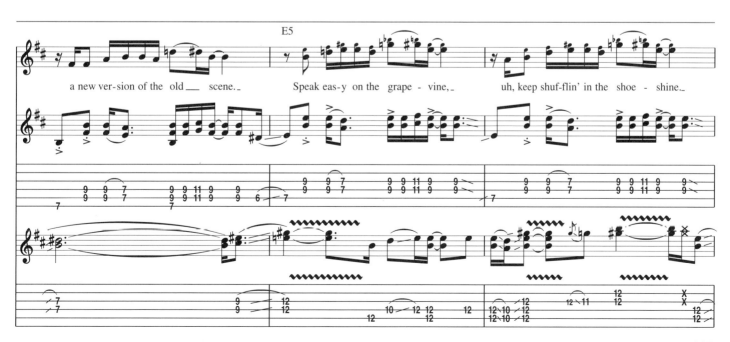

a new ver-sion of the old __ scene. __   Speak eas-y on the grape - vine, __   uh, keep shuf-flin' in the shoe - shine. __

Rag doll,   ba - by won't you do me, ba-by, won't you do me, ba-by won't you do me like you done be - fore, hoo, hoo.

Refugee

Words and Music by Tom Petty and Mike Campbell

don't have __ to live like a ref - u - gee.

(Don't have to live like a

Oh,   oh,   oh.

ref - u - gee.) __

Begin fade

Fade out

R.O.C.K. in the U.S.A.
(A Salute to 60's Rock)

Words and Music by John Mellencamp

118

With the pipe dreams in their heads and ver-y lit-tle mon-ey in ___ their hands.

Some are black ___ and some are white ___ and they

ain't too proud to sleep on your floor ___ to - night. ___ With the blind faith of Je - sus you

know that they ___ just might be rock-in' in the U. S.

Guitar Solo

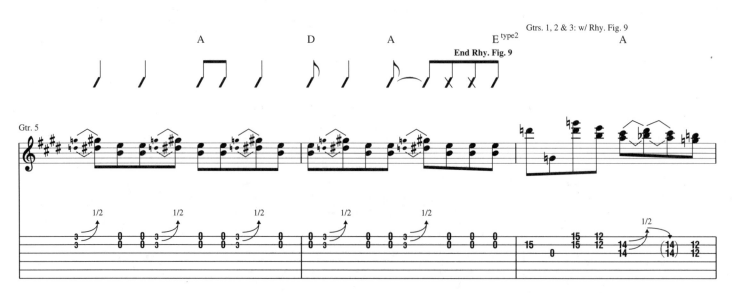

Young Ras - cals. (They were rock - in'.) Spot - light on Mar - tha Reeves. __ Let's don't for - get James

Brown. _____ Rock-in' in the U. S. A. _____ Hey!

Outro-Chorus

Gtrs. 1, 2 & 3: w/ Rhy. Figs. 6 & 6A

Gtrs. 1, 2 & 3: w/ Rhy. Figs. 7 & 7A (3 times)

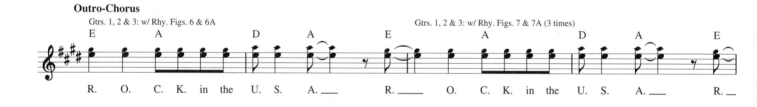

R. O. C. K. in the U. S. A. __ R. __ O. C. K. in the U. S. A. __ R. __

__ O. C. K. in the U. S. A. __ R. __ O. C. K. in the U. S. A. __ R. __

Repeat and fade

Gtrs. 1, 2 & 3: w/ Rhy. Figs. 7 & 7A (till fade)
Gtr. 5: w/ Rhy. Fig. 4A (till fade)

__ O. C. K. in the U. S. A. __ R. __ O. C. K. in the U. S. A. __ R. __

Rock Me

Words and Music by Alan Niven, Mark Kendall, Jack Russell and Michael Lardie

*Chord symbols reflect basic harmony.

**T = Thumb on 6th string

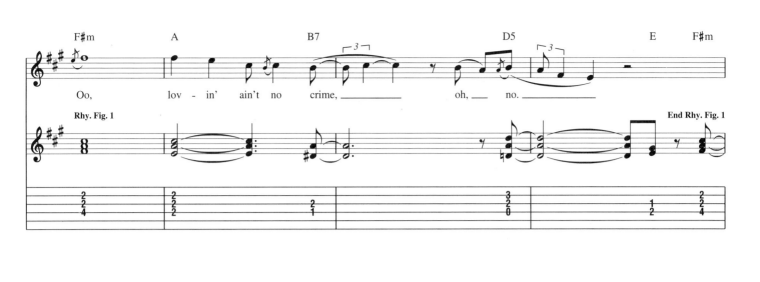

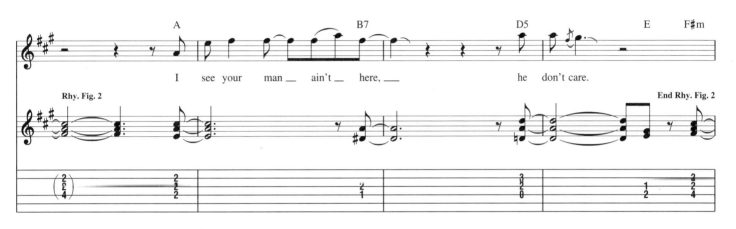

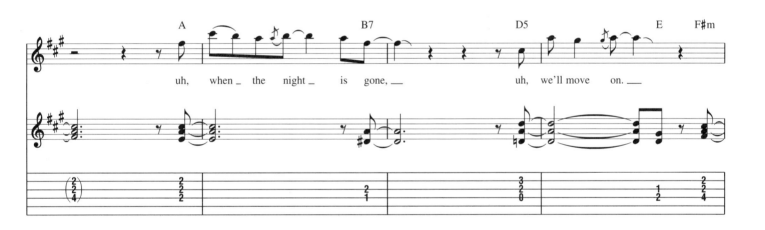

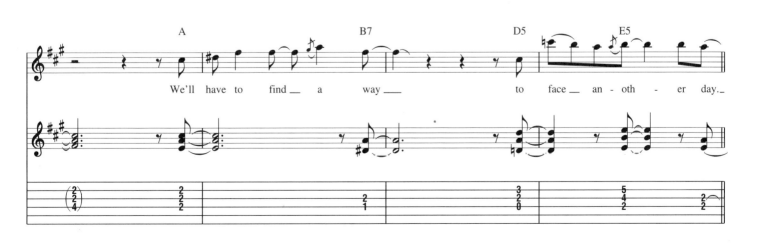

Interlude

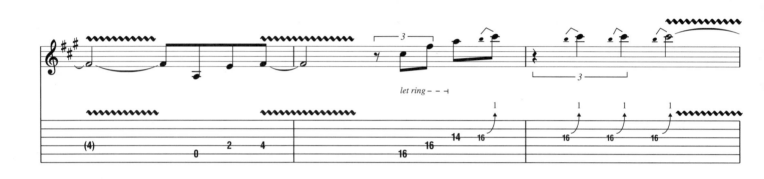

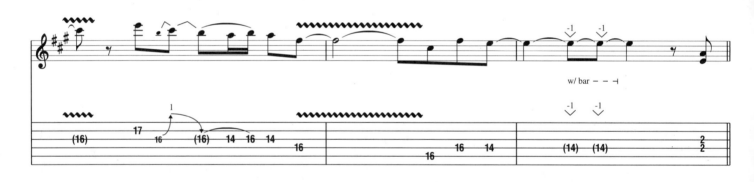

Verse

2. Search the world _ for some-one I'll nev-er find. _

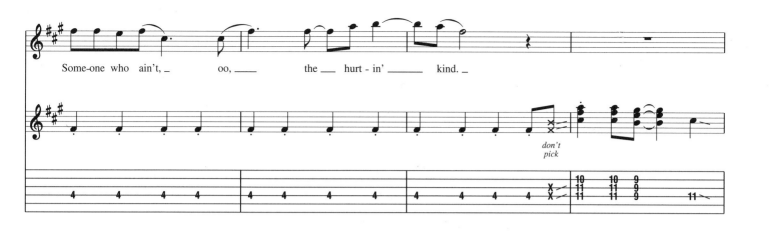

Some-one who ain't, _ oo, _ the _ hurt - in' _ kind. _

Gtr. 1: w/ Rhy. Fig. 1

F#m   A   B7   D5   E   F#m

Oo, _ if you stay _ the night, _ oh _ yeah. _

A   B7   D5   E5   F#5

we'll make the wrong_ seem right, _ so come on now. _ Rock _

Gtr. 1   Rhy. Fill 1   End Rhy. Fill 1

f

(cont. in slashes)

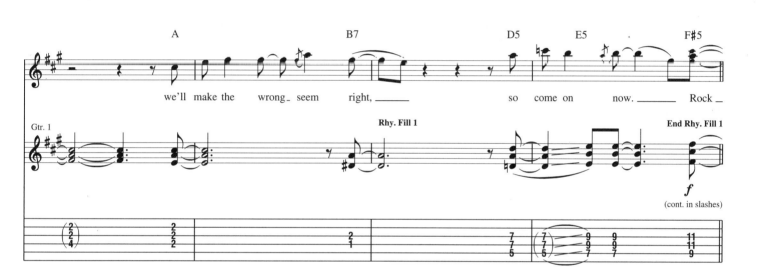

Chorus

F#5   C#5 D5   E5   D5   E5   F#5

Rhy. Fig. 3

Gtr. 1

(cont. in notation)

_ me, rock _ me, _ hold me through _ the night. _ Rock _

Rhy. Fig. 3A

*Gtrs. 2 & 3 (dist.)

f

*Composite arrangement

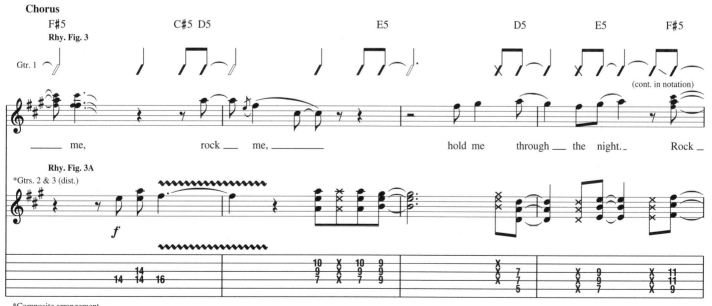

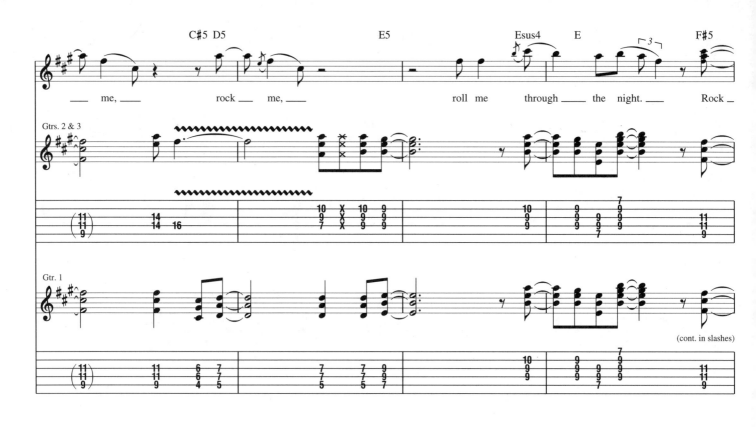

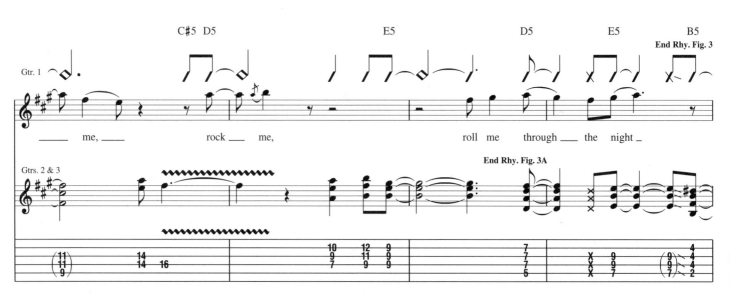

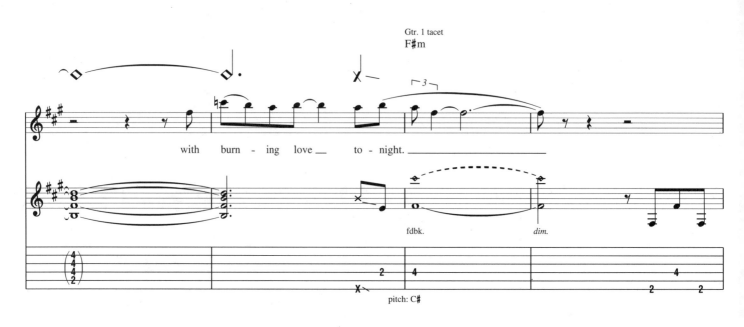

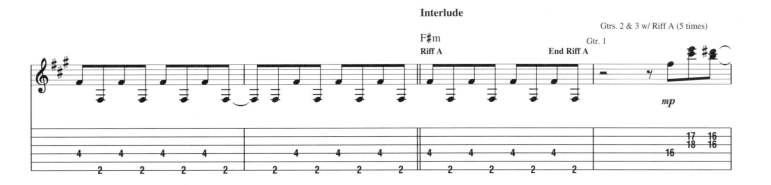

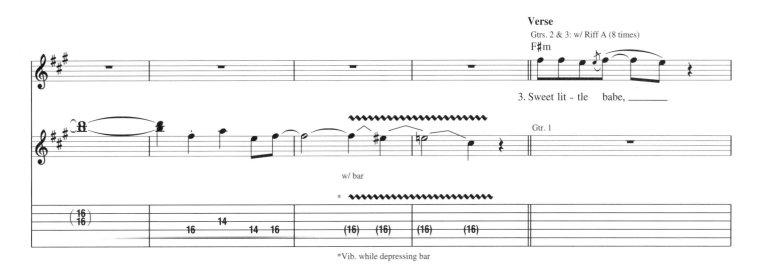

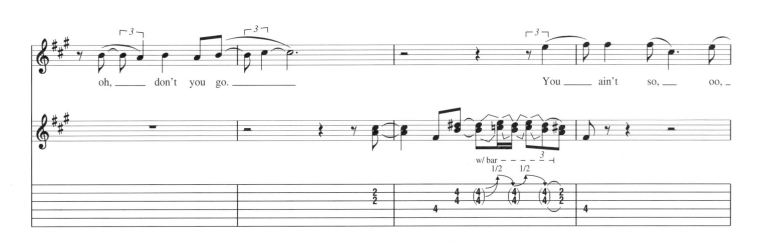

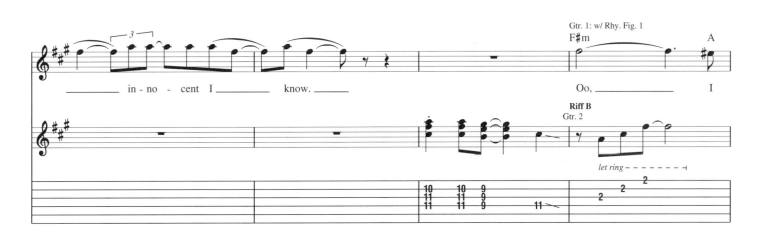

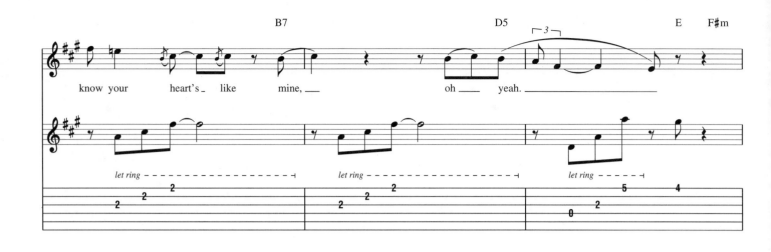

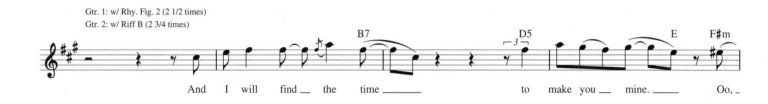

And I will find __ the time _____ to make you __ mine. _____ Oo, _

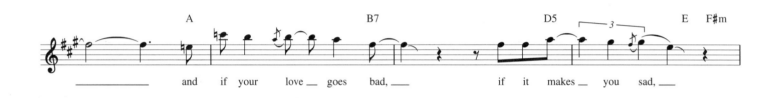

_____ and if your love __ goes bad, ___ if it makes __ you sad, __

and I'll be back __ for more, _____ hmm, at ___ your door. _____ Rock

Chorus

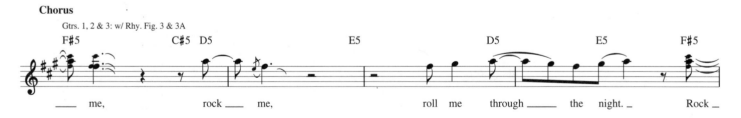

__ me, rock __ me, roll me through _____ the night. _ Rock _

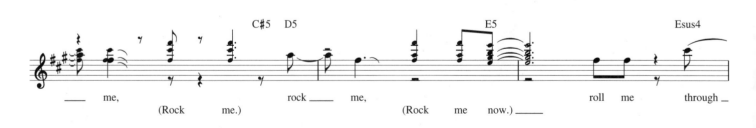

__ me, rock __ me, roll me through _
(Rock me.) (Rock me now.) _____

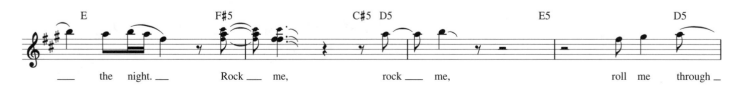

__ the night. __ Rock __ me, rock __ me, roll me through _

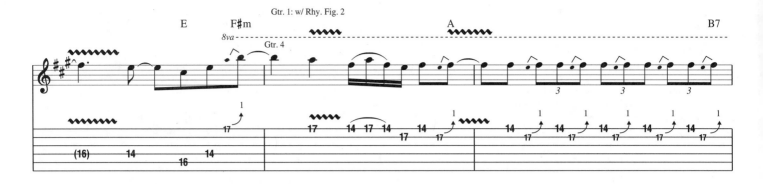

Verse

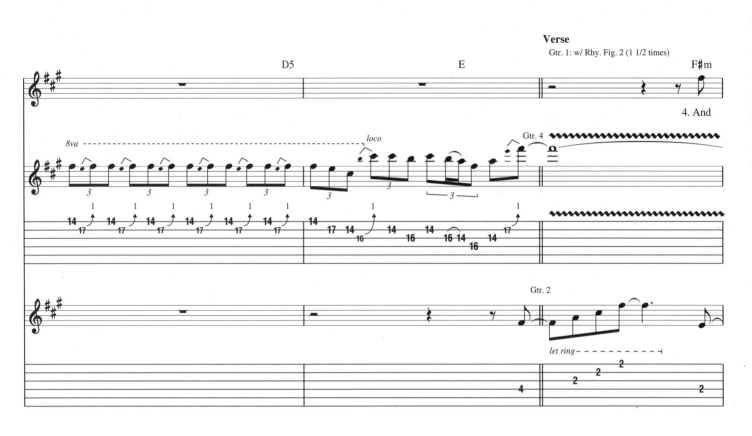

4. And

when your   man ___ don't   care, ___   I will ___   be   there. ___

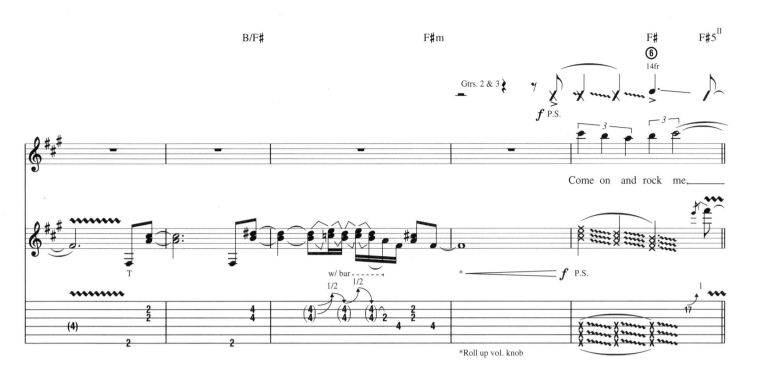

Come on and rock me,____

*Roll up vol. knob

Outro-Guitar Solo

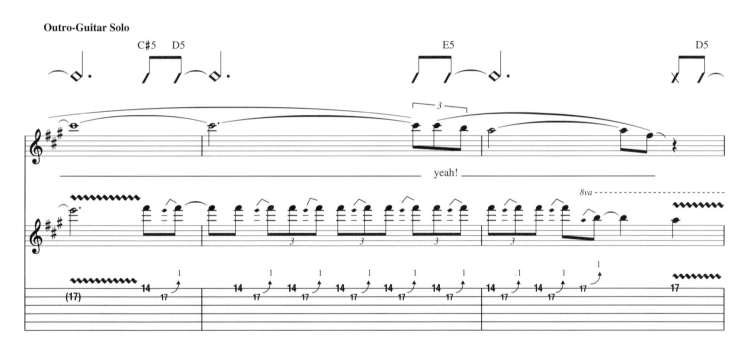

yeah!

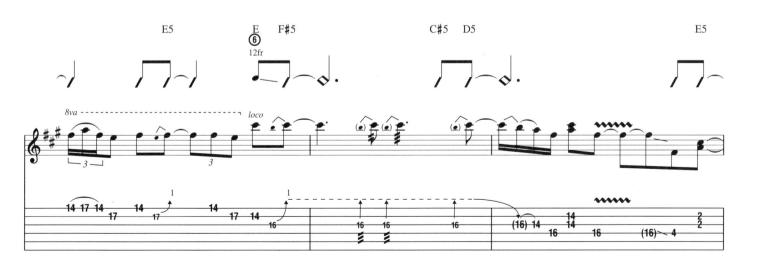

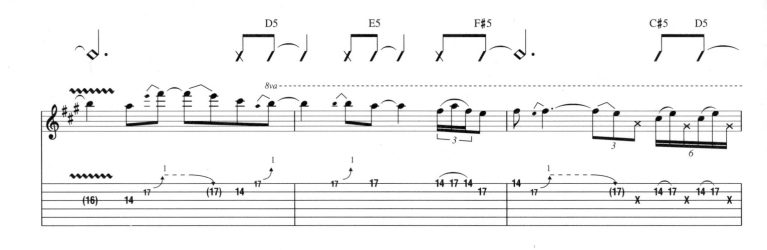
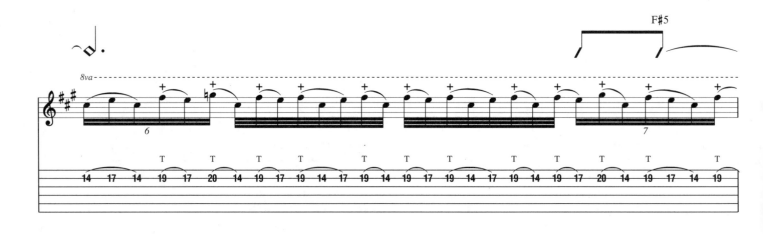
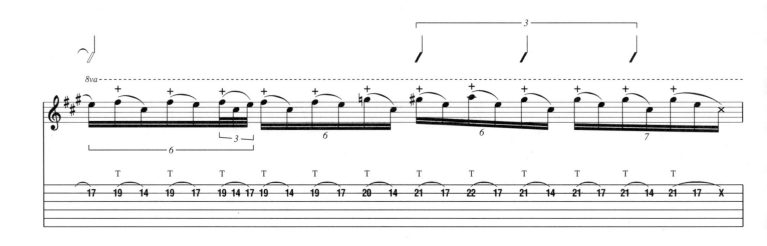

138

Rock You Like a Hurricane

Words and Music by Herman Rarebell, Klaus Meine and Rudolf Schenker

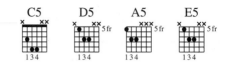

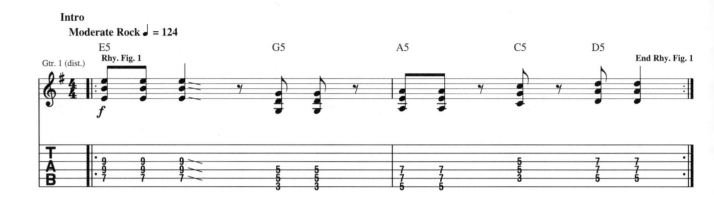

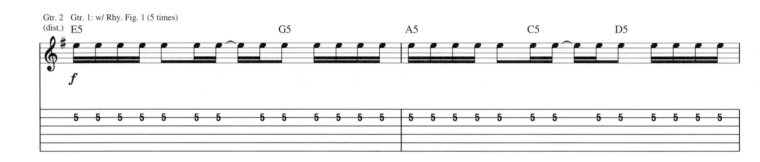

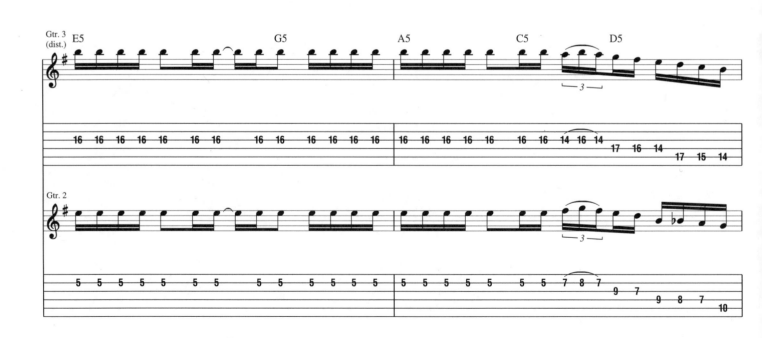

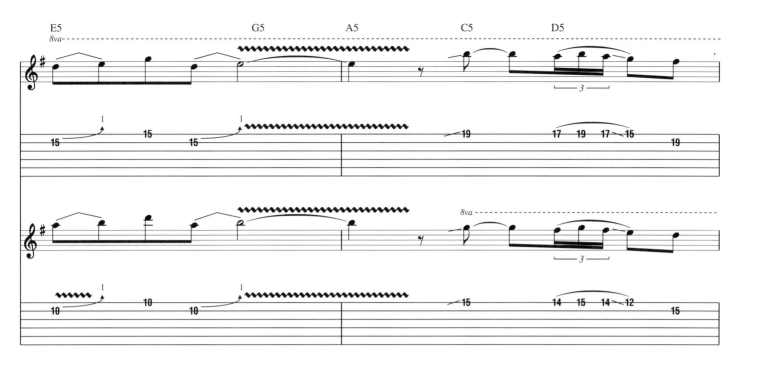

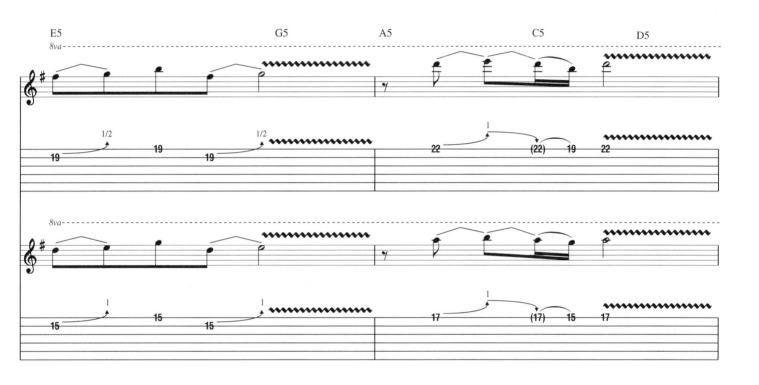

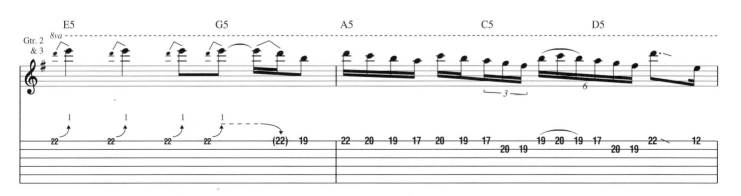

Here I am, rock __ you like a hur - ri - cane. ___

𝄉 Verse
Gtrs. 1 & 4: w/ Rhy. Fig. 2 (3 3/4 times)
2nd time, Gtrs. 1, 2 & 4 tacet

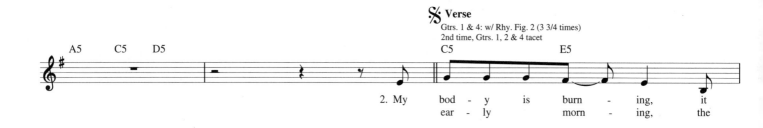

2. My bod - y is burn - ing, it
ear - ly morn - ing, the

starts to shout. __ De - sire's __ com - ing, it breaks out loud. __ Lust
sun comes out. __ Last night was shak - ing and pret - ty loud. __ My

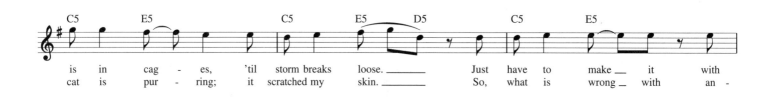

is in cag - es, 'til storm breaks loose. ___ Just have to make __ it with
cat is pur - ring; it scratched my skin. ___ So, what is wrong __ with an -

2nd time, Gtrs. 2 & 3: w/ Rhy. Fill 4   2nd time, Gtrs. 1 & 4: w/ Rhy. Fig. 2 (1 3/4 times)

some - one I choose.. __ } The night is call - ing, I have to go. ___ The wolf is hun - gry, he
oth - er sin? __ }

* Gtr. 2 & 3

* Composite arrangement

Rhy. Fill 4
Gtrs. 2 & 3

Here I am, rock _ you like a hur-ri-cane. Come on, come on, come on, come on. _

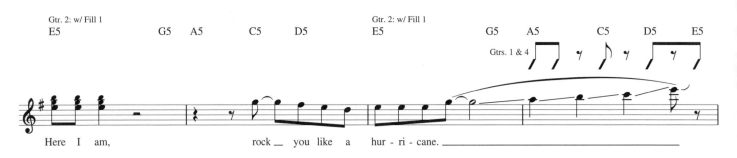

Here I am, rock _ you like a hur-ri-cane. _

Guitar Solo
Gtr. 1: w/ Rhy. Fig. 1 (7 1/2 times)
Gtr. 4 tacet

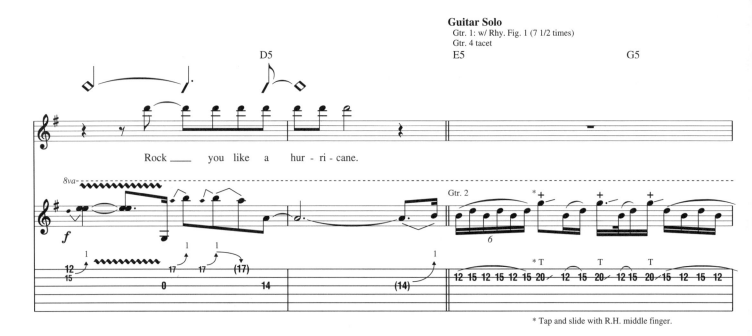

Rock _ you like a hur-ri-cane.

* Tap and slide with R.H. middle finger.

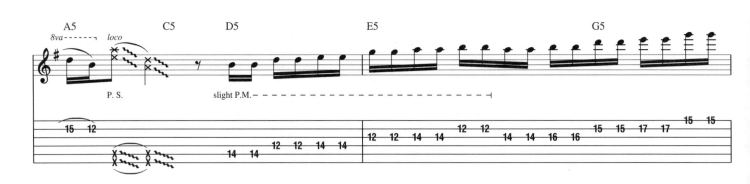

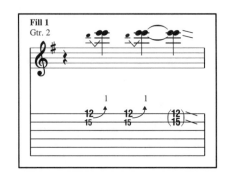

Fill 1
Gtr. 2

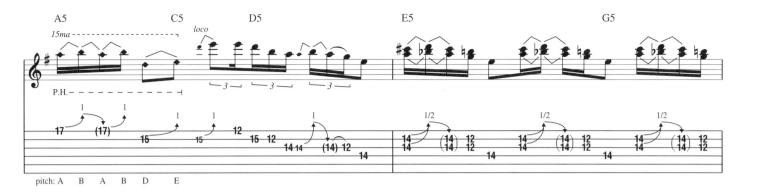

pitch: A B A B D E

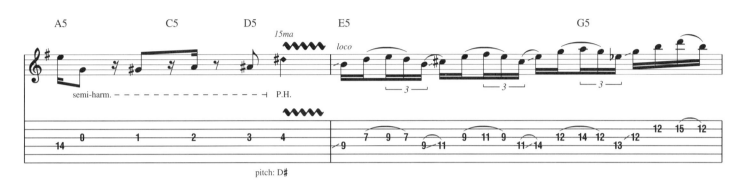

pitch: D♯

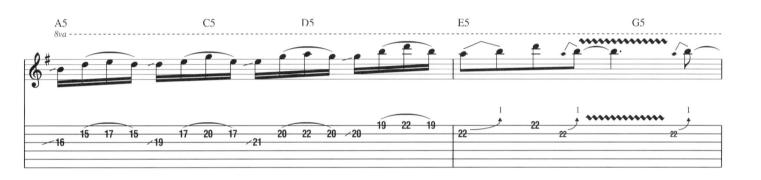

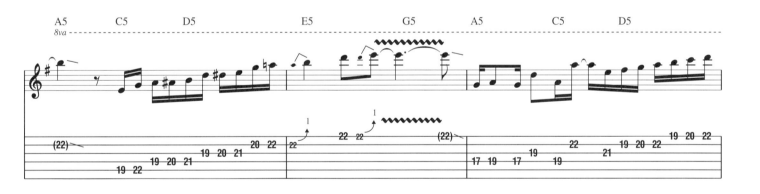

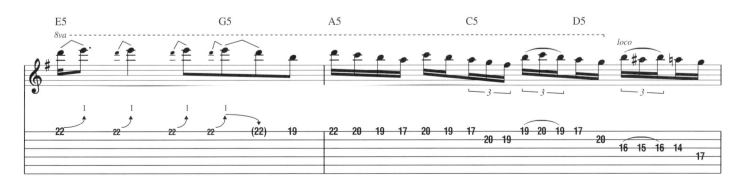

3. It's

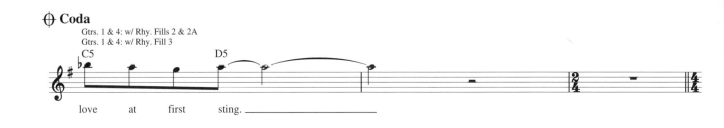

love at first sting. ___

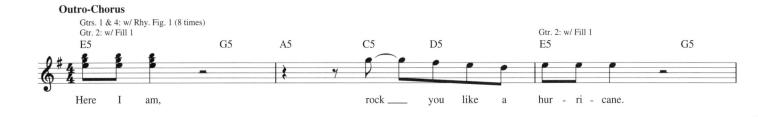

Here I am, rock ___ you like a hur - ri - cane.

Are you read - y ba - by? ___ Here I am, rock ___ you like a

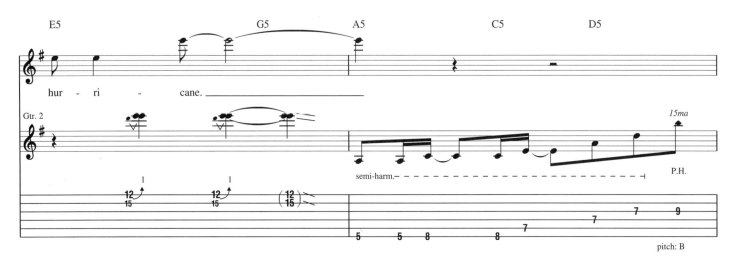

hur - ri - cane. ___

Running on Faith

Words and Music by Jerry Williams

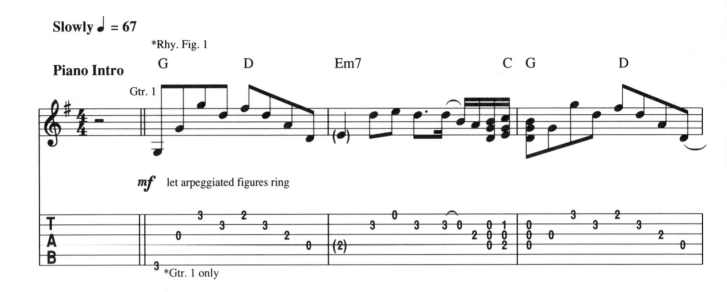

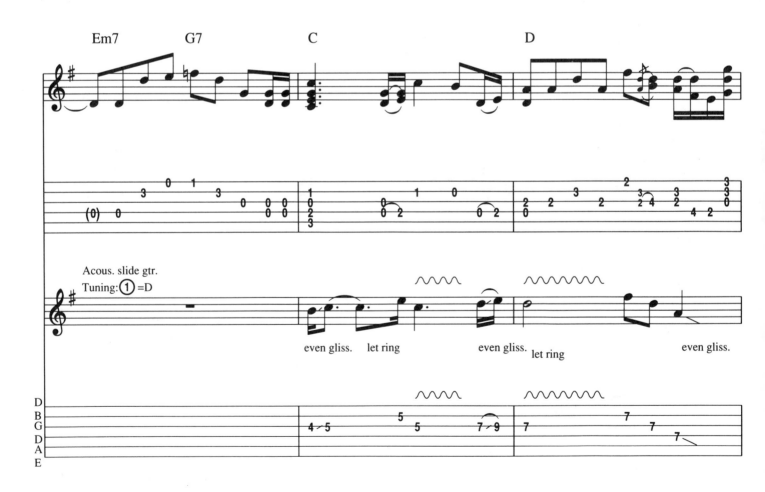

1. Late– ly I've been run–nin'on ___ faith.___

let ring

*1/4

let ring

*slide extra 1/4 step

___ What else ___ can a poor ___ boy ___ do? ___

1st Verse

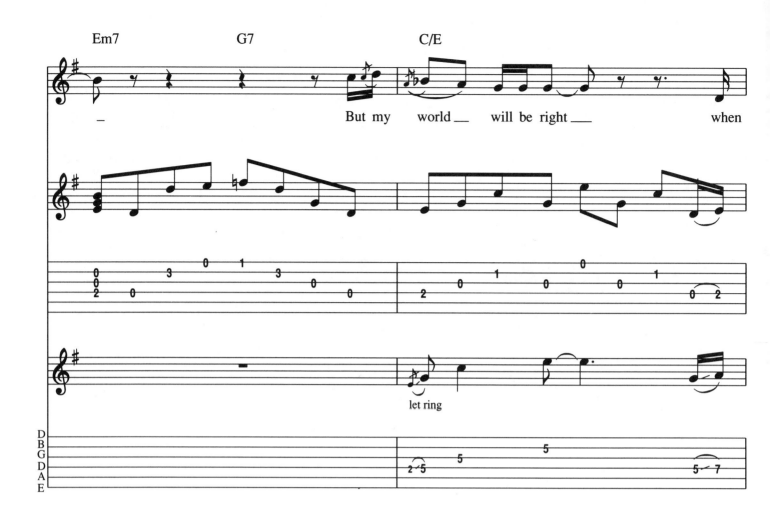

But my world ___ will be right ___ when

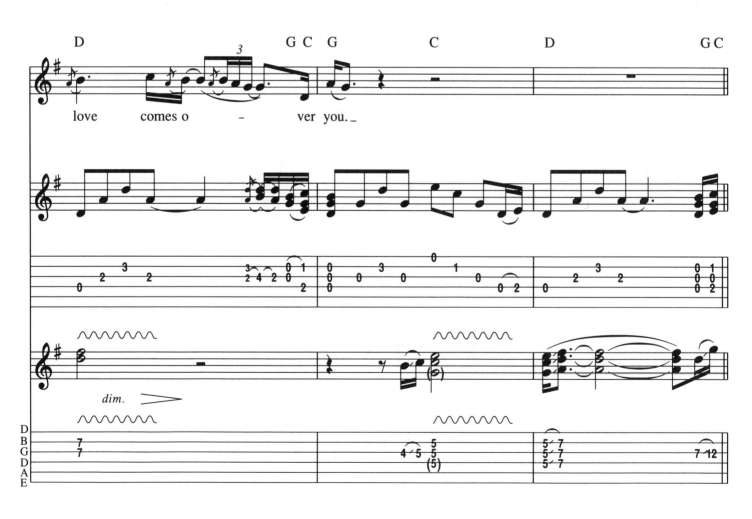

love comes o - ver you. _

2nd Verse

2. Late–ly I've been talk-in'in___ my sleep. Can't i-ma-gine what I have _ to say._

'Cept my world_ will be right, _ when love. comes back_ your

way. _____ I've _ al- ways

been one to take _ each and ev- 'ry day. _

154

Seems _____ like 'bout now _____ I'd find a love _who cares just for

3rd Verse

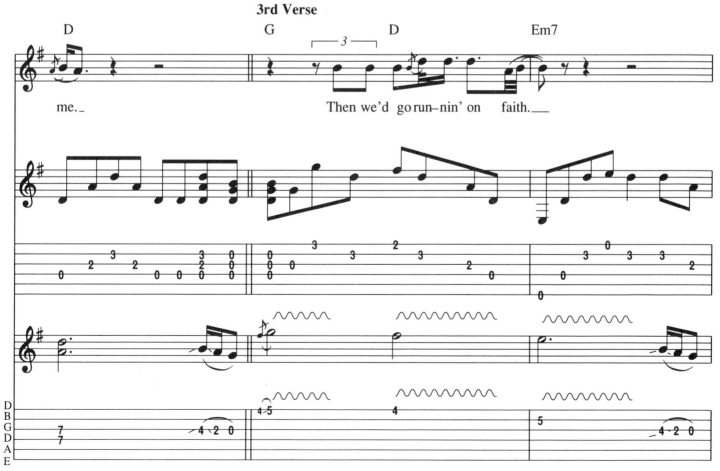

me._ Then we'd go run–nin' on faith.__

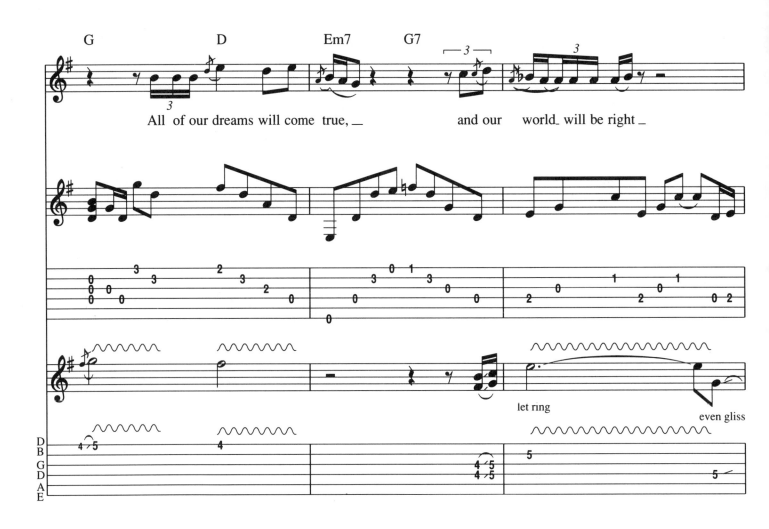

All of our dreams will come true, _____ and our world _ will be right _

when love _ comes o - ver me and you. _____

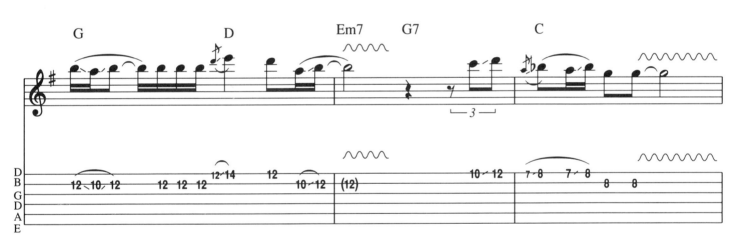

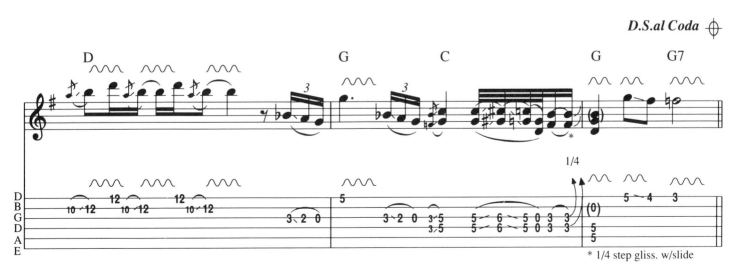

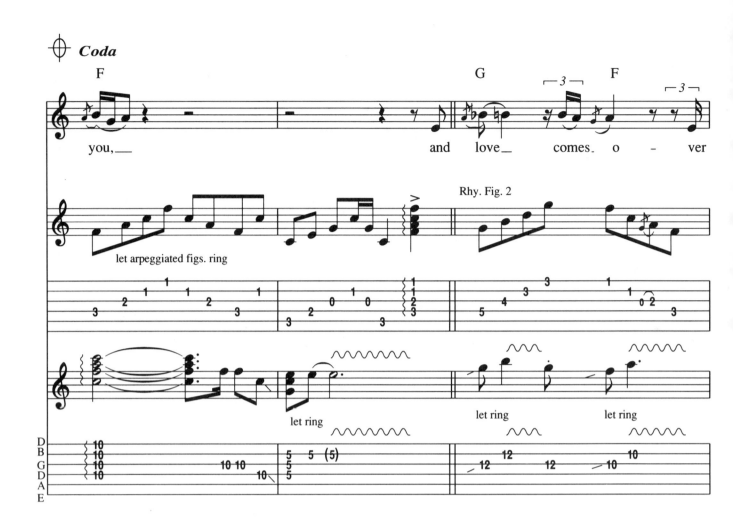

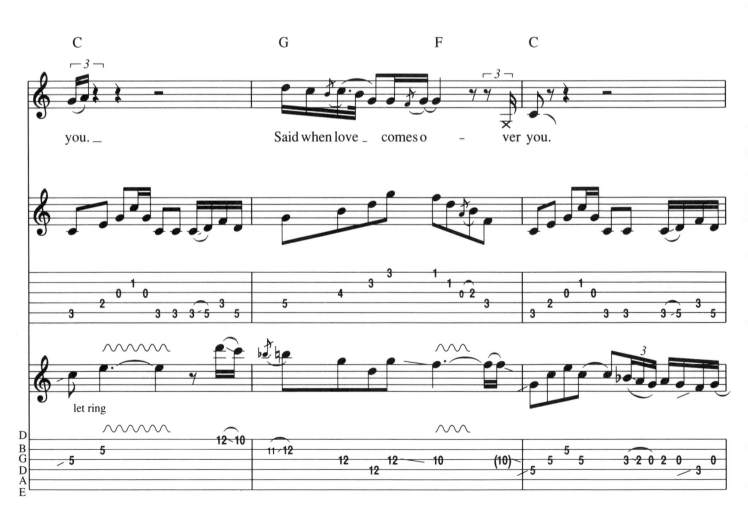

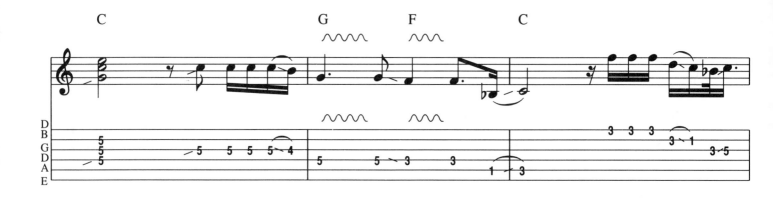

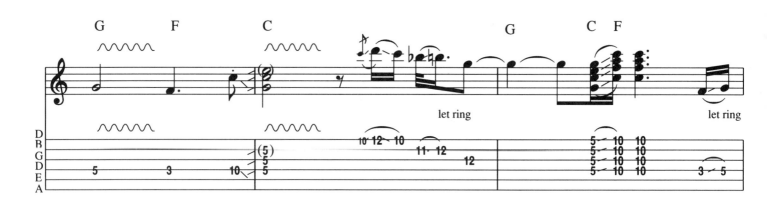

Rubato

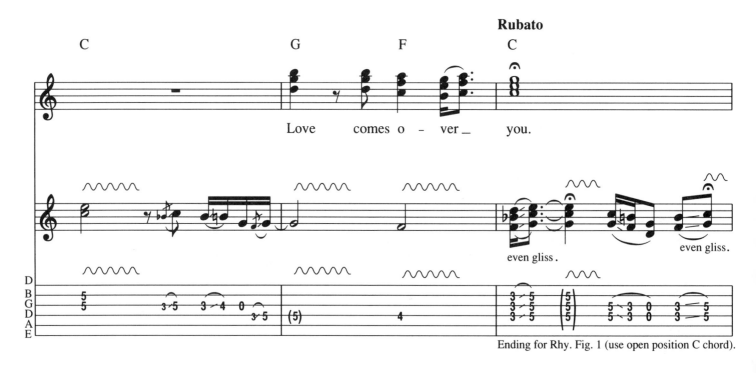

Love comes o - ver _ you.

let ring

let ring

even gliss.

even gliss.

Ending for Rhy. Fig. 1 (use open position C chord).

N.C.

even gliss.

Seventeen

Words and Music by Kip Winger, Reb Beach and Beau Hill

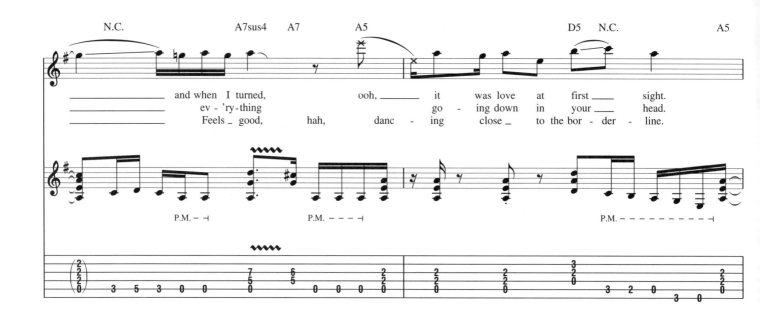

and when I turned, ooh, it was love at first sight.
ev - 'ry-thing go - ing down in your head.
Feels good, hah, danc - ing close to the bor - der - line.

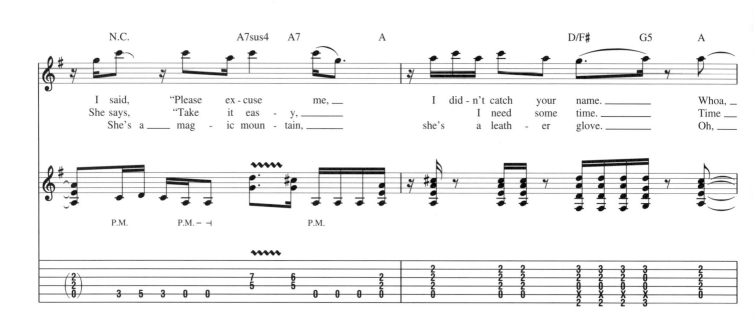

I said, "Please ex - cuse me, I did - n't catch your name. Whoa,
She says, "Take it eas - y, I need some time. Time
She's a mag - ic moun - tain, she's a leath - er glove. Oh,

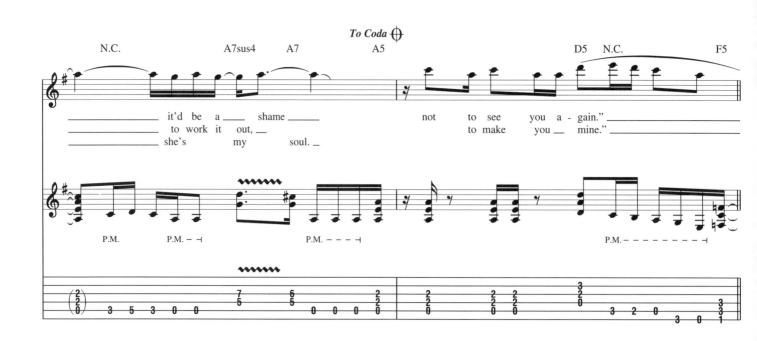

it'd be a shame not to see you a - gain."
to work it out, to make you mine."
she's my soul.

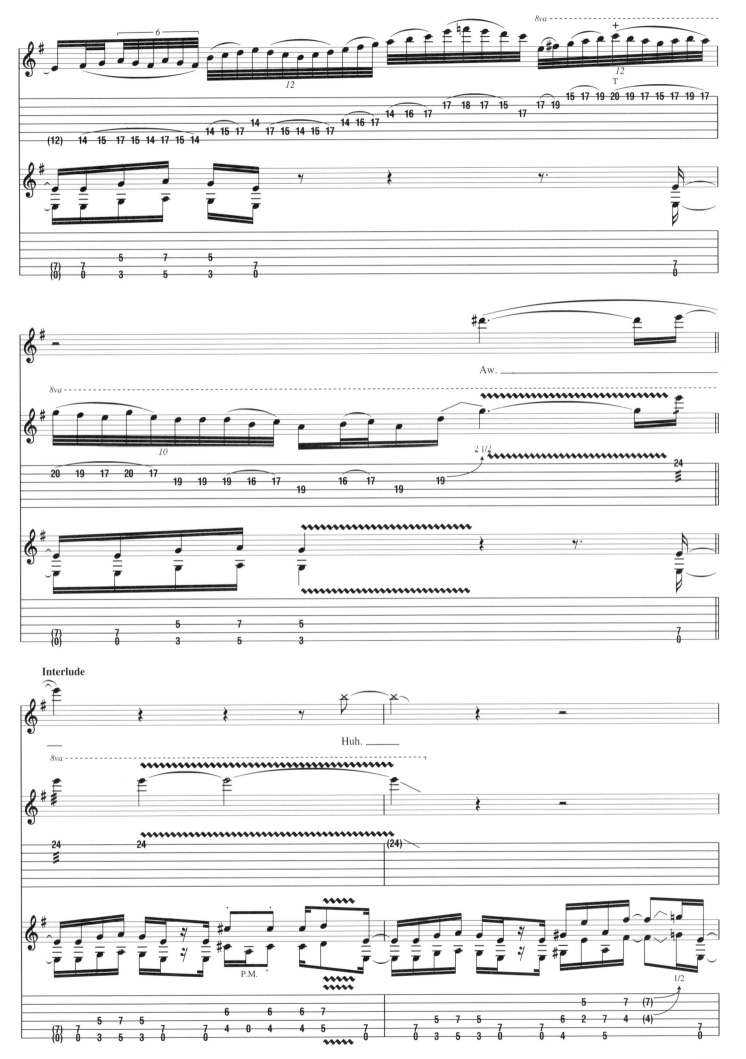

Outro Guitar Solo

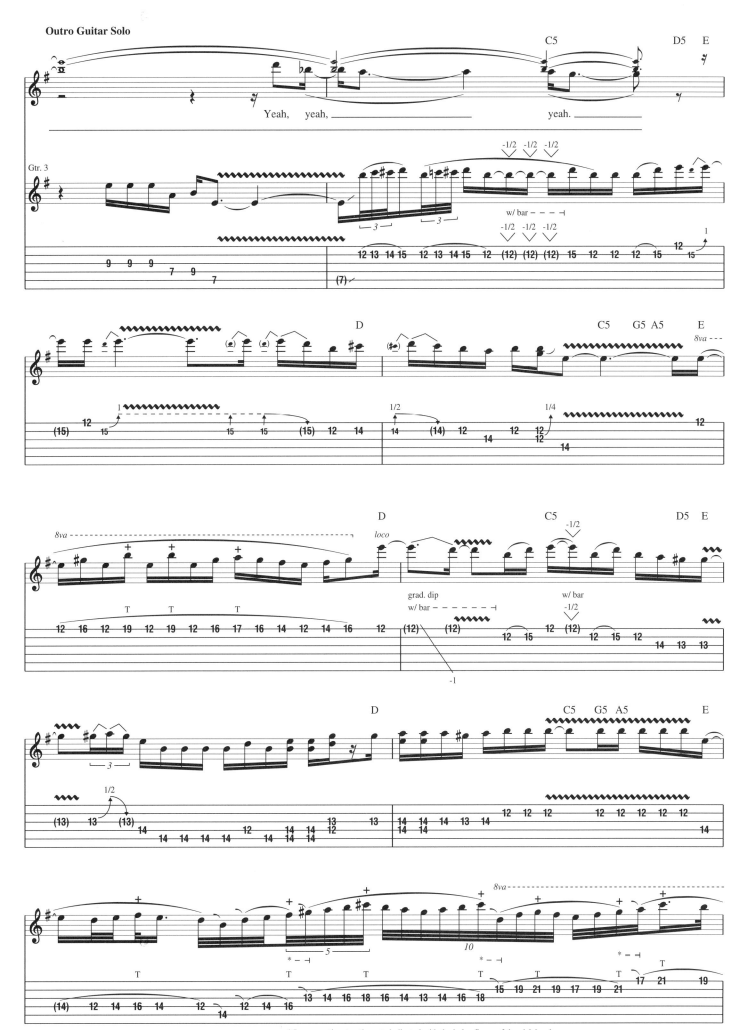

Yeah, yeah, _____ yeah. _____

* In one motion, tap the note indicated with the index finger of the pick hand,
then pluck the adjacent strings with the same finger while pulling off.

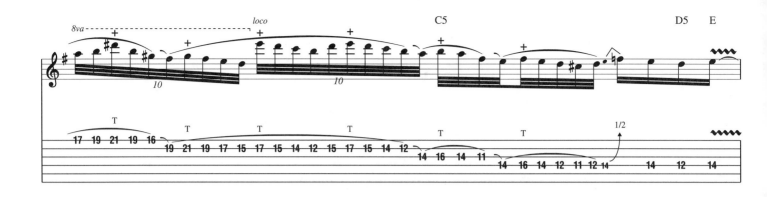

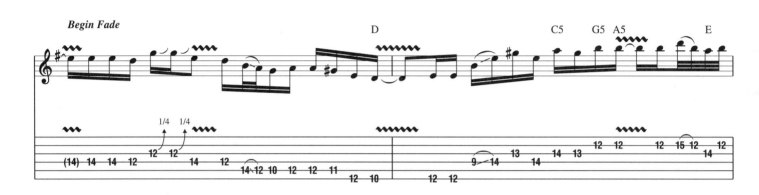

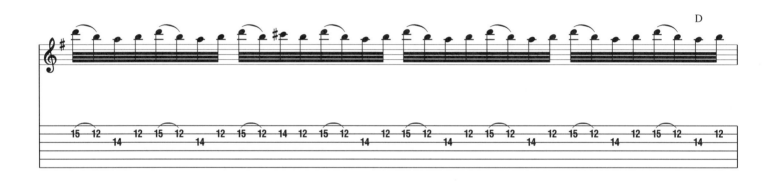

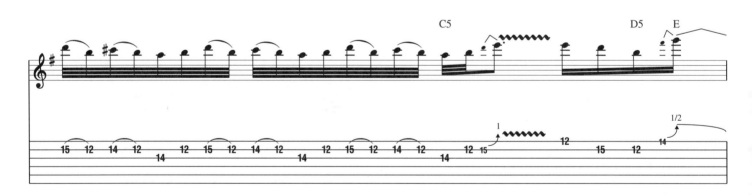

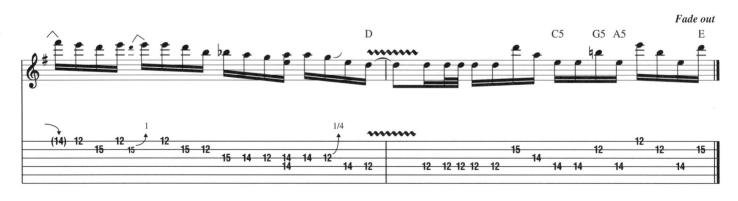

Start Me Up

Words and Music by Mick Jagger and Keith Richards

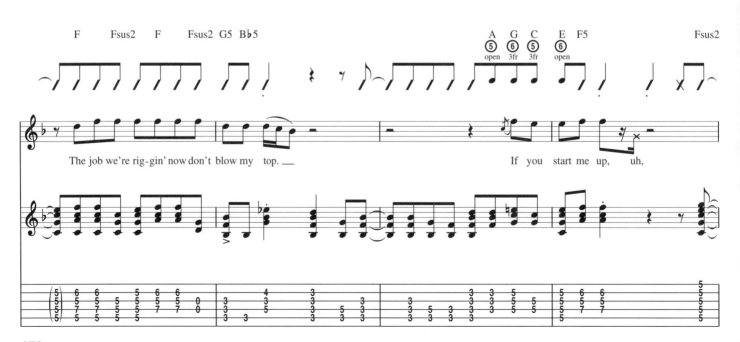

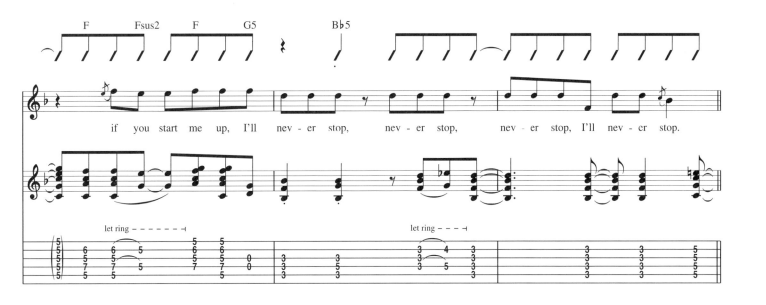

Chorus

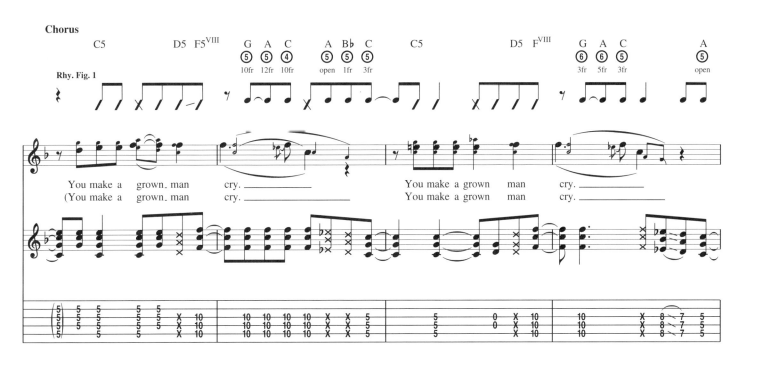

You make a grown man cry. ____ You make a grown man cry. ____
(You make a grown man cry. ____ You make a grown man cry. ____

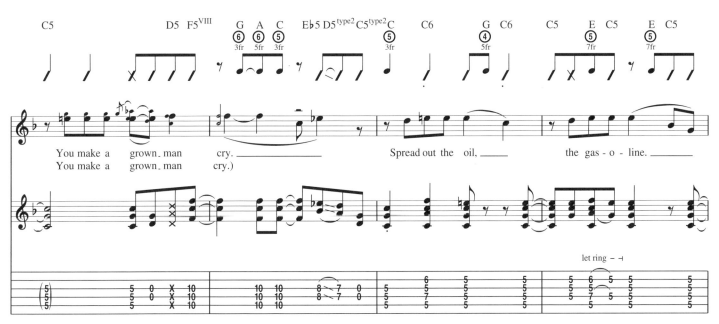

You make a grown man cry. ____ Spread out the oil, ____ the gas-o-line. ____
You make a grown man cry.)

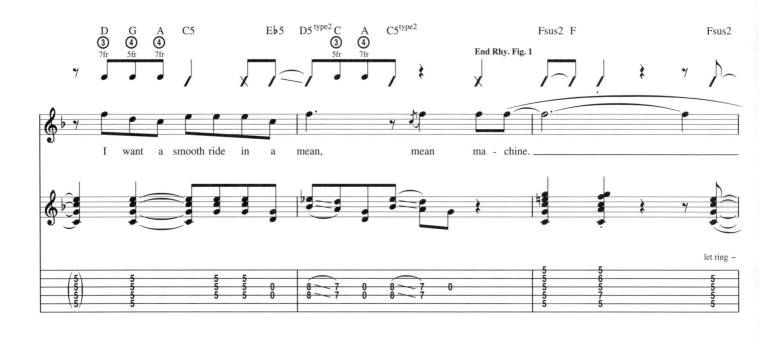

174

Chorus

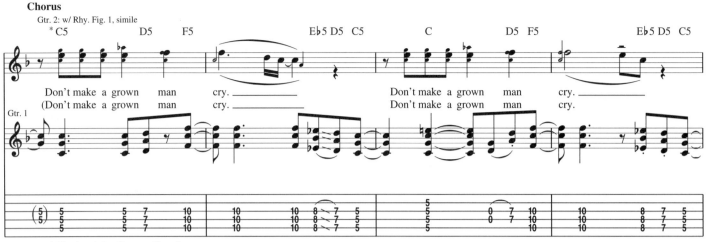

Gtr. 2: w/ Rhy. Fig. 1, simile

* C5   D5   F5   Eb5 D5 C5   C   D5   F5   Eb5 D5 C5

Don't make a grown man cry. _____

(Don't make a grown man cry. _____

Don't make a grown man cry.

Don't make a grown man cry.

Gtr. 1

* Chord symbols reflect overall tonality.

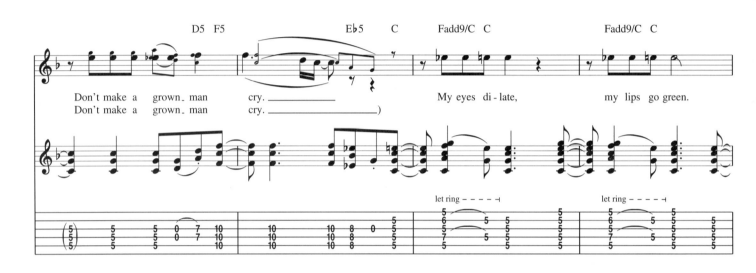

D5   F5   Eb5   C   Fadd9/C   C   Fadd9/C   C

Don't make a grown man cry. _____

Don't make a grown man cry. _____)

My eyes di-late, my lips go green.

let ring ----

let ring ----

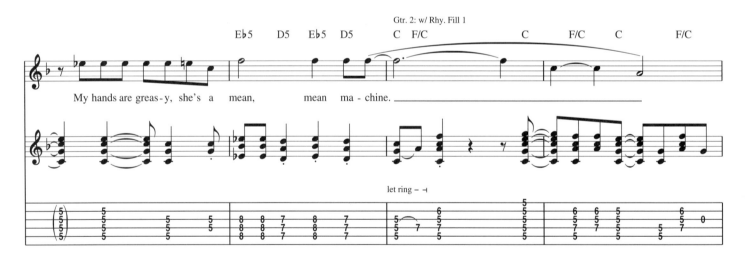

Gtr. 2: w/ Rhy. Fill 1

Eb5   D5   Eb5   D5   C   F/C   C   F/C   C   F/C

My hands are greas-y, she's a mean, mean ma-chine. _____

let ring --

Rhy. Fill 1

Gtr. 2

176

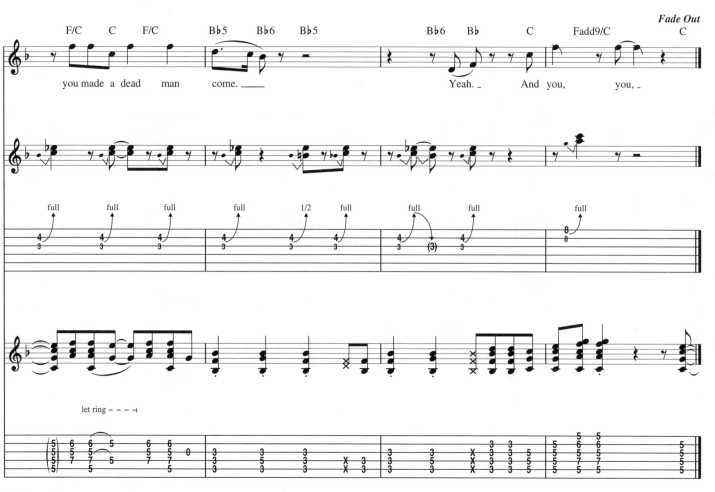

180

Summer of '69

Words and Music by Bryan Adams and Jim Vallance

Gtr. 4: w/ Rhy. Fig. 4

Dsus2 D Dsus4 D Dsus2 D Asus2 A Asus4 A Asus2 A

Verse

Gtrs. 1, 2 & 3: w/ Riffs A & A1 (2 times)
Gtr. 4: w/ Rhy. Fig. 4 (1st 2 meas.)

Dsus2 D Dsus4 D Dsus2 D Asus2 A Asus4 A Asus2 A

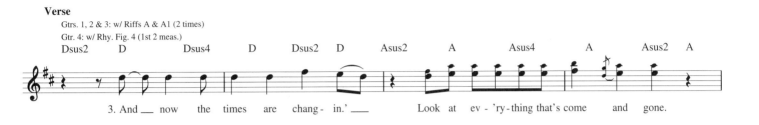

3. And __ now the times are chang- in.' __ Look at ev - 'ry-thing that's come and gone.

D.S. al Coda 2

Dsus2 D Dsus4 D Dsus2 D Asus2 A Asus4 A Asus2 A

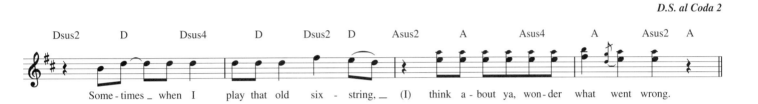

Some - times _ when I play that old six - string, _ (I) think a - bout ya, won - der what went wrong.

$\oplus$ **Coda 2**

Outro-Chorus

Gtrs. 1, 2 & 3: w/ Riffs A & A1 (till end)
Gtr. 4: w/ Rhy. Fig. 4 (till end)

Dsus2 D Dsus4 D Dsus2 D Asus2 A Asus4 A Asus2 A

life. Oh, __ yeah. __ Back in the sum - mer of

Dsus2 D Dsus4 D Dsus2 D Asus2 A Asus4 A Asus2 A

six - ty - nine. __ Uh, huh. __ It was the sum - mer of

Dsus2 D Dsus4 D Dsus2 D Asus2 A Asus4 A Asus2 A

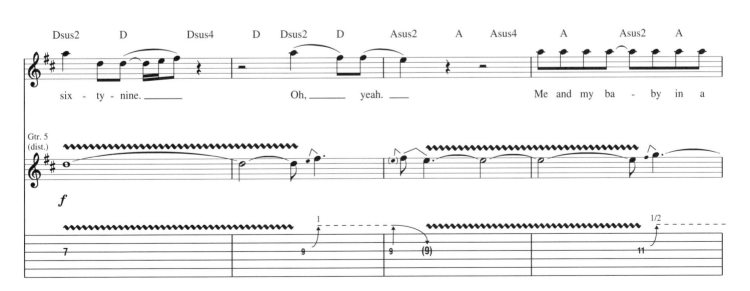

six - ty - nine. ___ Oh, ___ yeah. __ Me and my ba - by in a

Gtr. 5
(dist.)

f

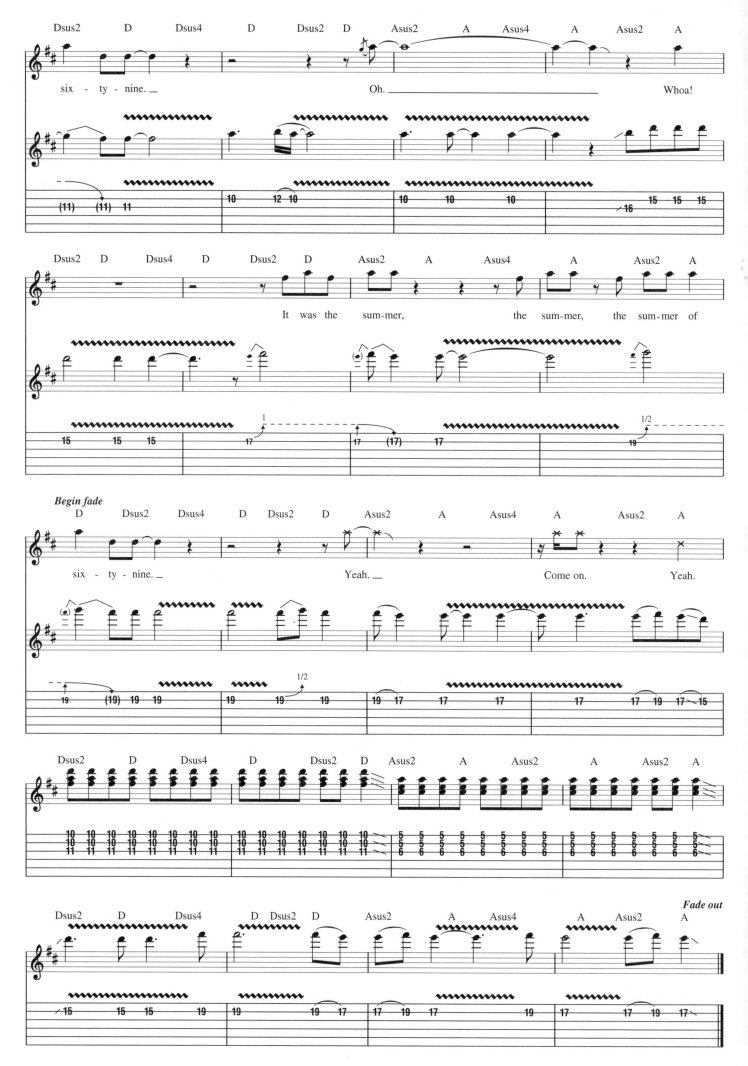

Sweet Child O' Mine

Words and Music by W. Axl Rose, Slash, Izzy Stradlin', Duff McKagan and Steven Adler

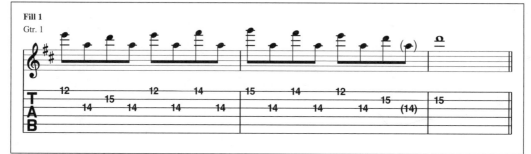

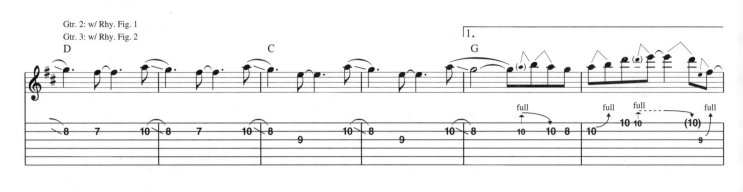

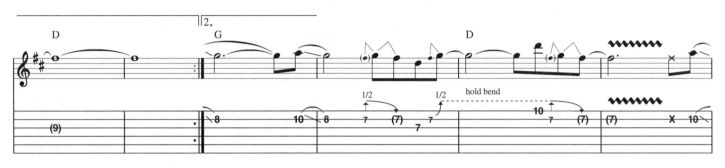

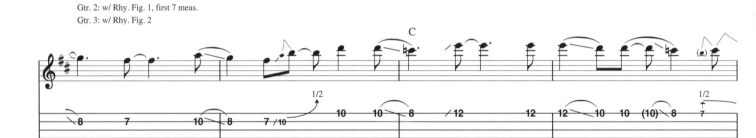

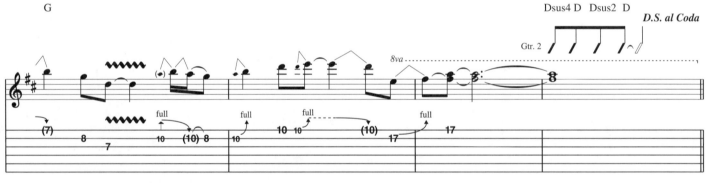

Oh, oh, — oh, oh, _____ sweet child _ o' mine.

Woo, ___ yeah, _ yeah! Ooh, _____ sweet love o' mine. _____

Guitar Solo

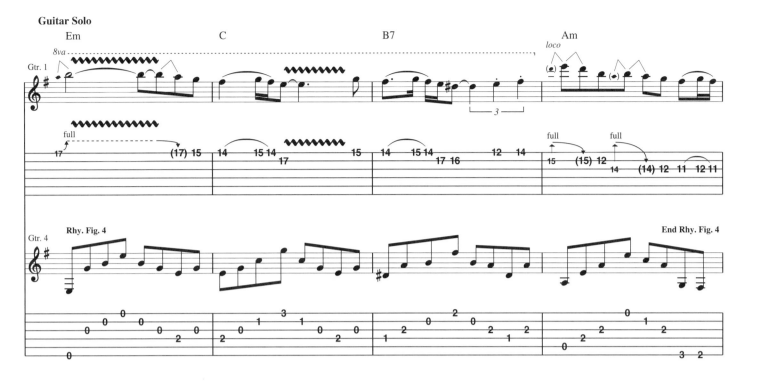

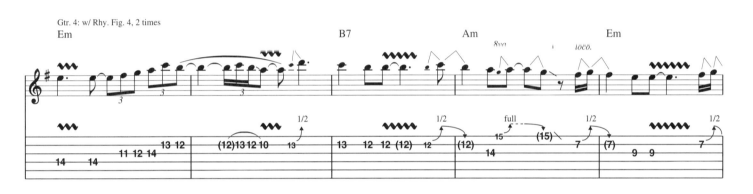

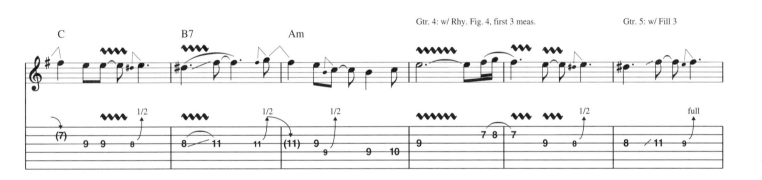

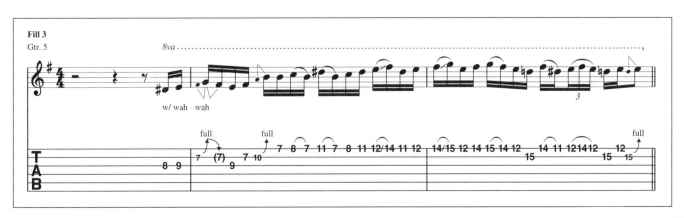

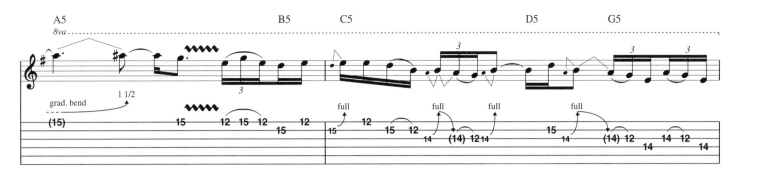

Gtr. 2: w/ Rhy. Fig. 6, 2 times

Where do we go? __ Where do we go __ now? Where do we go? __ Where do we go? __

Where do we go __ now? Where do we go? __ Where do we go? __ (whispered) Sweet Child!

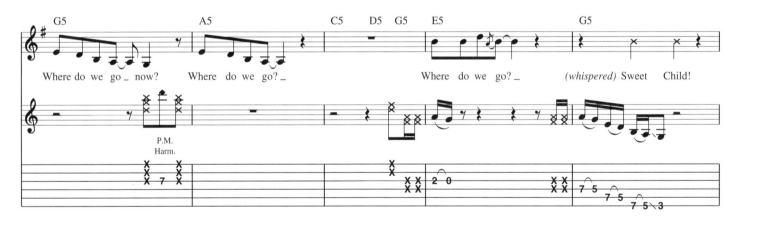

Where do we go __ now?

I, I, I, I,

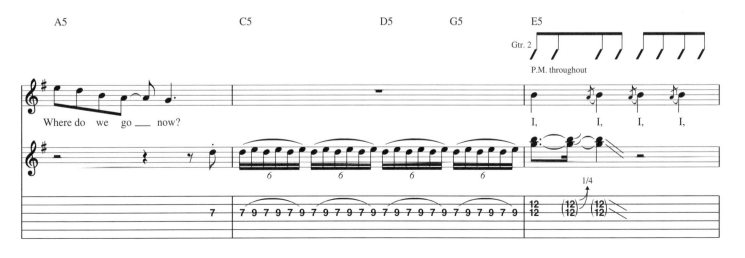

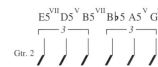

Where do we go? ____   Where do we go ___ now?   No, no, no, no, no, no,

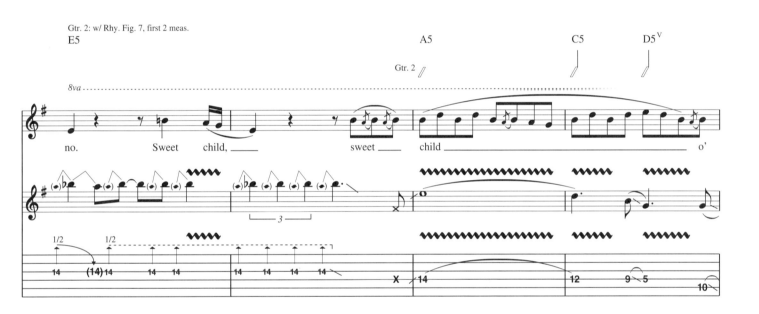

no.   Sweet   child, _____   sweet ___ child _____ o'

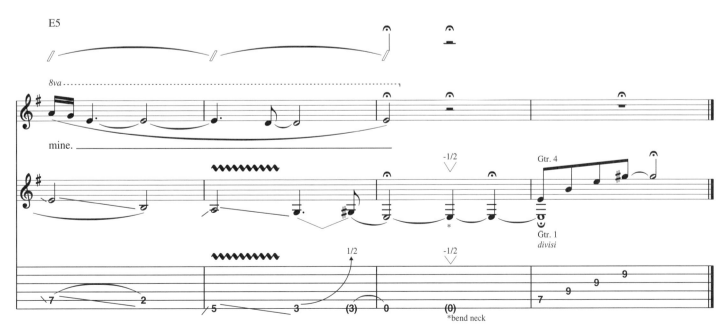

mine. _____

Wait

Words and Music by Mike Tramp and Vito Bratta

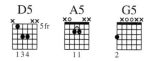

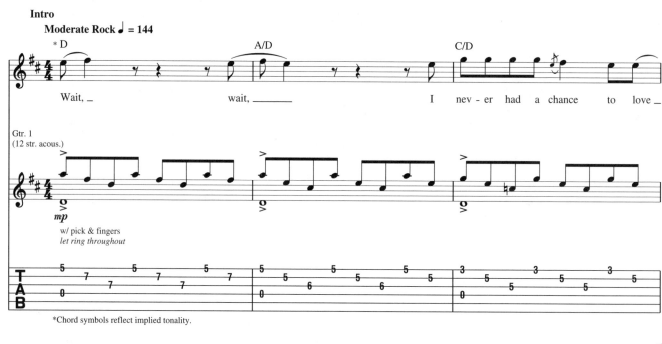

*Chord symbols reflect implied tonality.

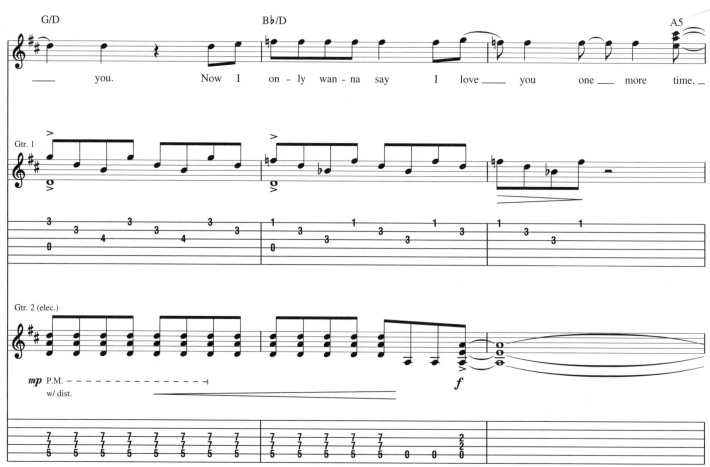

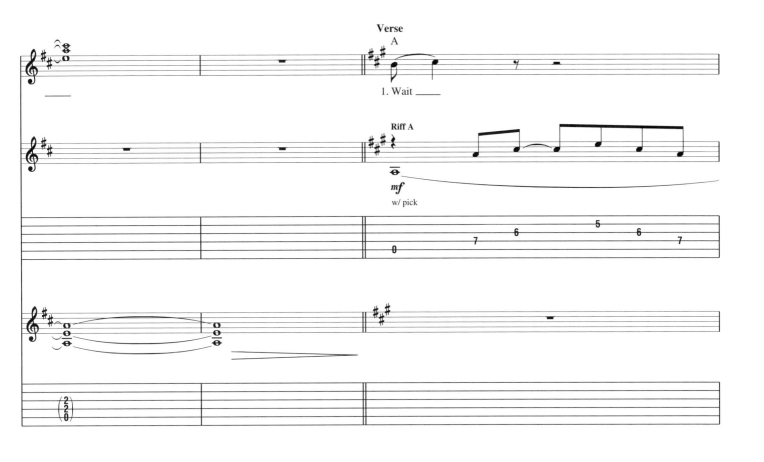

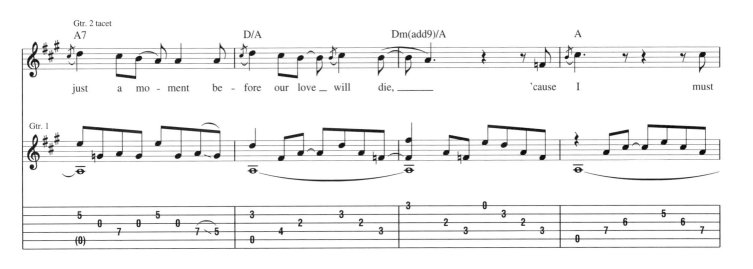

198

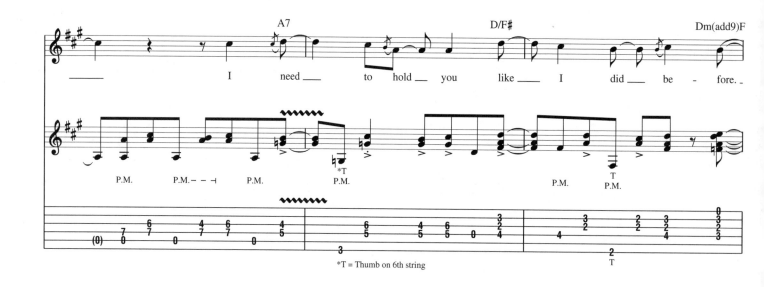

Pre-Chorus
2nd time, Gtr. 4 tacet

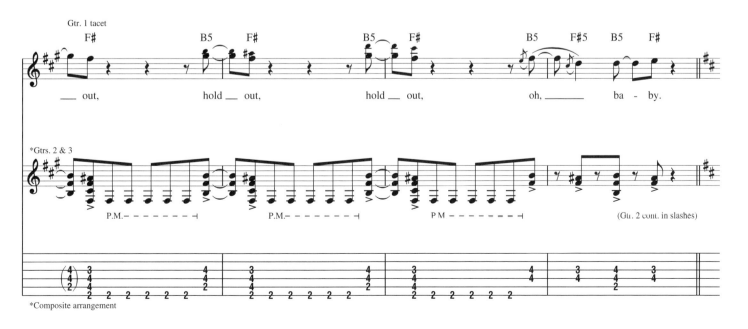

Chorus

Wait,   wait, _____   I nev-er had a chance to love __ you.

Wait,   wait, _____   if on-ly our love could show __ you.

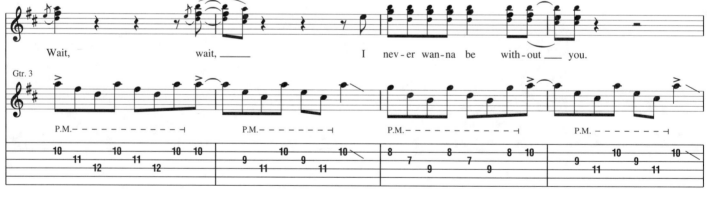

Wait,   wait, _____   I nev-er wan-na be with-out __ you.

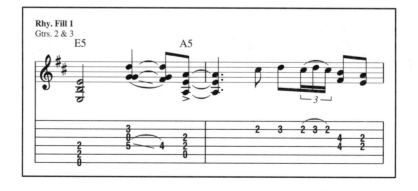

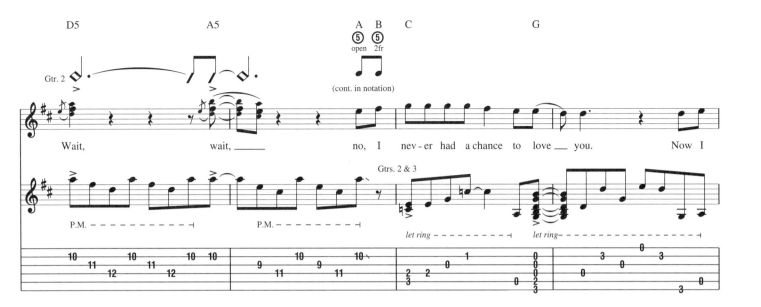

Wait, wait, _____ no, I nev-er had a chance to love _____ you. Now I

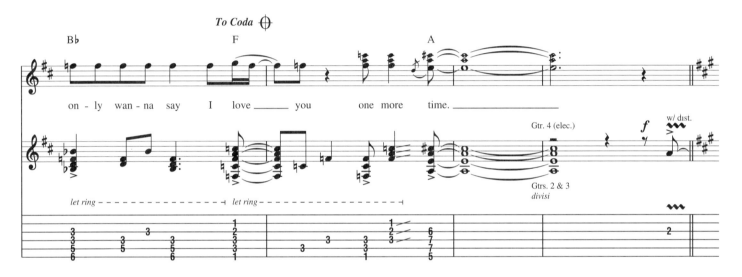

on-ly wan-na say I love _____ you one more time.

Guitar Solo

Gtr. 1: w/ Riff A
Gtrs. 2 & 3 tacet

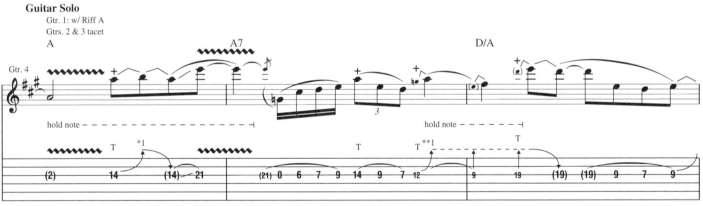

*Bend and vibrato are executed by left hand, fingered at 3rd str., 2nd fr.

**Bend w/ left hand at 3rd str., 9 fr.

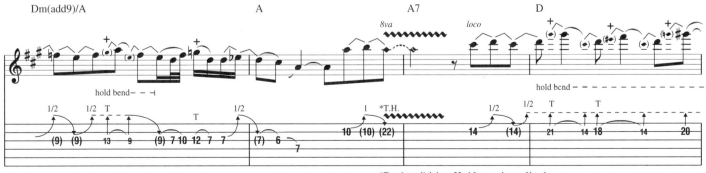

*Touch str. lightly at 22nd fret at release of bend.

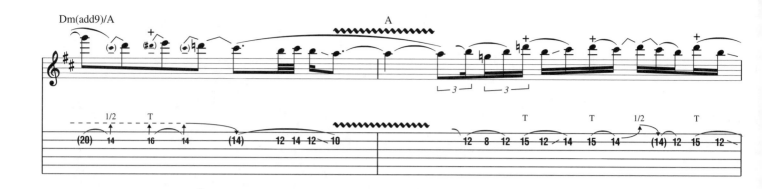

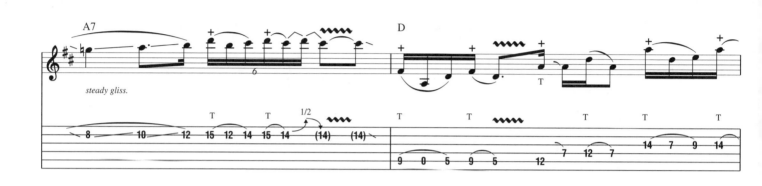

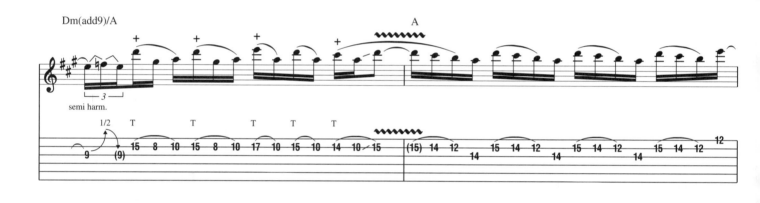

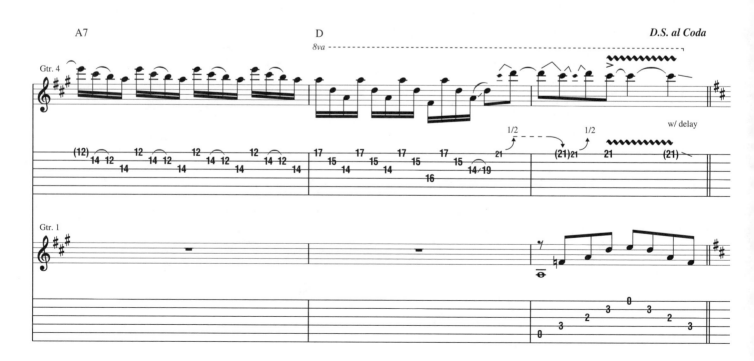

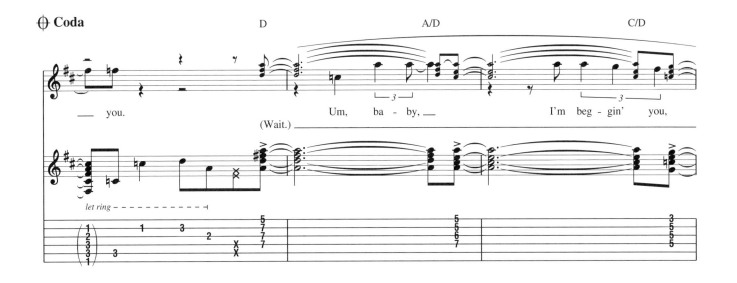

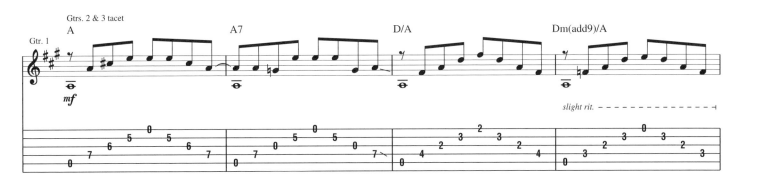

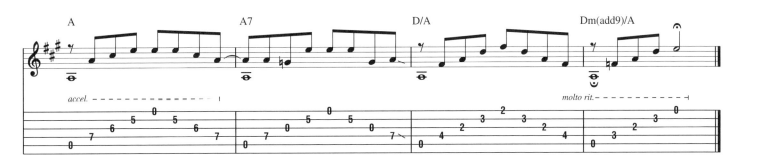

What I Like About You

Words and Music by Michael Skill, Wally Palamarchuk and James Marinos

Working for the Weekend

Words and Music by Paul Dean, Matthew Frenette and Michael Reno

Chorus

You bet-ter start from the start. _____

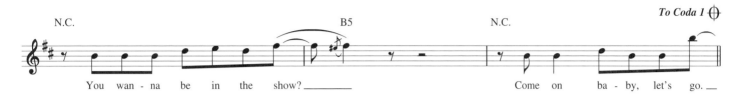

You wan-na be in the show? _____ Come on ba - by, let's go. _____

Interlude

Verse

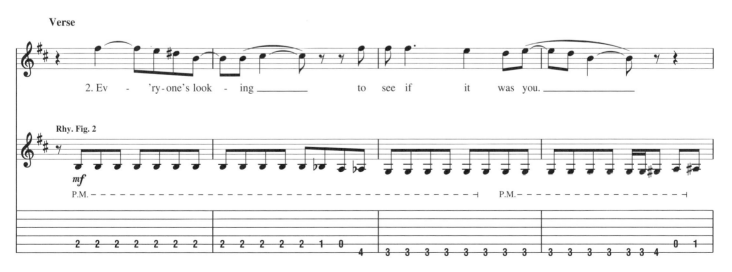

2. Ev - 'ry-one's look - ing _____ to see if it was you. _____

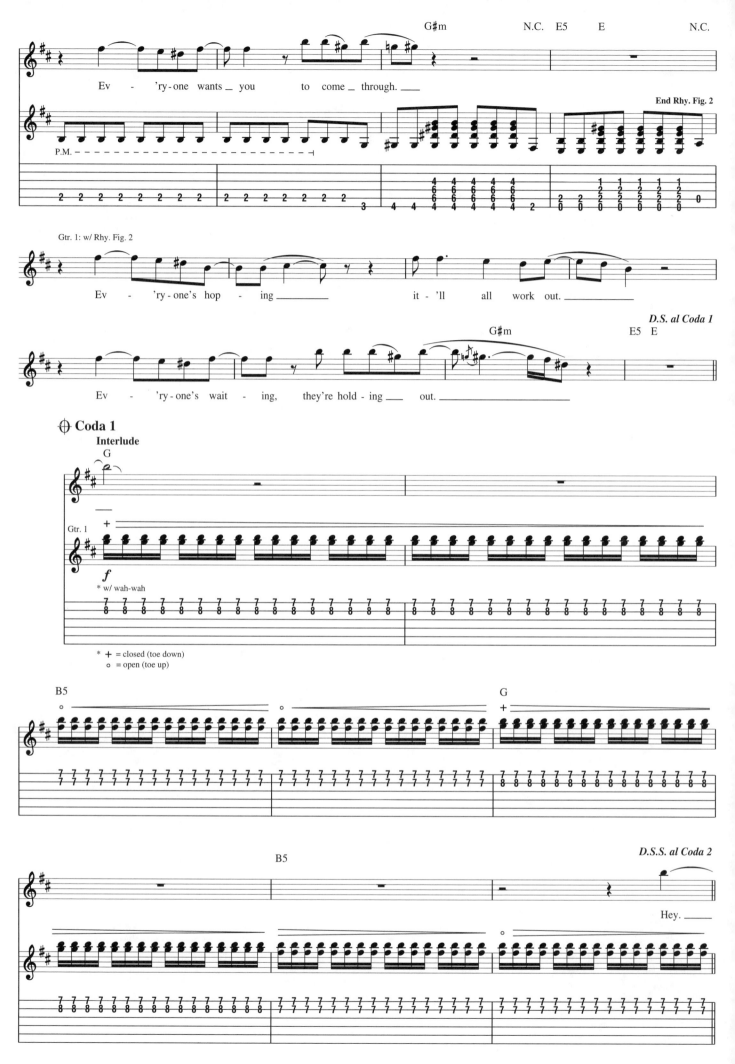

You May Be Right

Words and Music by Billy Joel

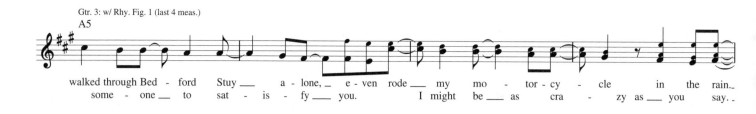

walked through Bed - ford Stuy ___ a - lone, e - ven rode ___ my mo - tor - cy - cle in the rain.
some - one ___ to sat - is - fy ___ you. I might be ___ as cra - zy as ___ you say.

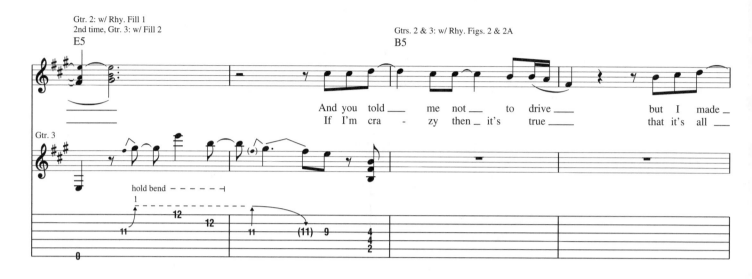

Gtr. 2: w/ Rhy. Fill 1
2nd time, Gtr. 3: w/ Fill 2

E5

Gtrs. 2 & 3: w/ Rhy. Figs. 2 & 2A

B5

And you told ___ me not ___ to drive ___ but I made ___
If I'm cra - zy then ___ it's true ___ that it's all ___

Gtr. 3

hold bend

G5

E5

___ it home ___ a - live, ___ so you said ___ that on - ly proves ___ that I'm ___ in -
___ be - cause ___ of you, ___ and you would - n't want ___ me an - y oth - er

𝄋 **Chorus**
3rd time, Gtr. 6 tacet

A5   A

Gtr. 2

E5

Gtr. 3

sane. ___
way. ___

You may ___ be right, ___ I may ___ be cra -

* Gtrs. 3 & 4

* Composite arrangement; Gtr. 4 (dist.) *mf*

Fill 2
Gtr. 3

* 2nd & 3rd times, this chord is omitted.

Guitar Notation Legend

Guitar Music can be notated three different ways: on a *musical staff*, in *tablature*, and in *rhythm slashes*.

RHYTHM SLASHES are written above the staff. Strum chords in the rhythm indicated. Use the chord diagrams found at the top of the first page of the transcription for the appropriate chord voicings. Round noteheads indicate single notes.

THE MUSICAL STAFF shows pitches and rhythms and is divided by bar lines into measures. Pitches are named after the first seven letters of the alphabet.

TABLATURE graphically represents the guitar fingerboard. Each horizontal line represents a a string, and each number represents a fret.

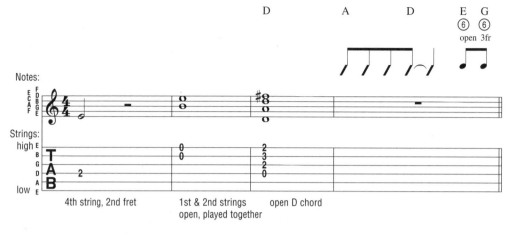

4th string, 2nd fret

1st & 2nd strings open, played together

open D chord

Definitions for Special Guitar Notation

HALF-STEP BEND: Strike the note and bend up 1/2 step.

WHOLE-STEP BEND: Strike the note and bend up one step.

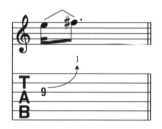

GRACE NOTE BEND: Strike the note and immediately bend up as indicated.

SLIGHT (MICROTONE) BEND: Strike the note and bend up 1/4 step.

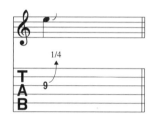

BEND AND RELEASE: Strike the note and bend up as indicated, then release back to the original note. Only the first note is struck.

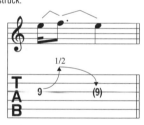

PRE-BEND: Bend the note as indicated, then strike it.

PRE-BEND AND RELEASE: Bend the note as indicated. Strike it and release the bend back to the original note.

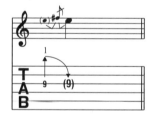

UNISON BEND: Strike the two notes simultaneously and bend the lower note up to the pitch of the higher.

VIBRATO: The string is vibrated by rapidly bending and releasing the note with the fretting hand.

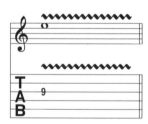

WIDE VIBRATO: The pitch is varied to a greater degree by vibrating with the fretting hand.

HAMMER-ON: Strike the first (lower) note with one finger, then sound the higher note (on the same string) with another finger by fretting it without picking.

PULL-OFF: Place both fingers on the notes to be sounded. Strike the first note and without picking, pull the finger off to sound the second (lower) note.

LEGATO SLIDE: Strike the first note and then slide the same fret-hand finger up or down to the second note. The second note is not struck.

SHIFT SLIDE: Same as legato slide, except the second note is struck.

TRILL: Very rapidly alternate between the notes indicated by continuously hammering on and pulling off.

TAPPING: Hammer ("tap") the fret indicated with the pick-hand index or middle finger and pull off to the note fretted by the fret hand.

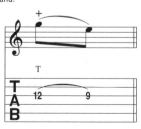

NATURAL HARMONIC: Strike the note while the fret-hand lightly touches the string directly over the fret indicated.

PINCH HARMONIC: The note is fretted normally and a harmonic is produced by adding the edge of the thumb or the tip of the index finger of the pick hand to the normal pick attack.

HARP HARMONIC: The note is fretted normally and a harmonic is produced by gently resting the pick hand's index finger directly above the indicated fret (in parentheses) while the pick hand's thumb or pick assists by plucking the appropriate string.

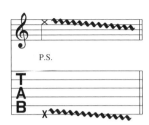

PICK SCRAPE: The edge of the pick is rubbed down (or up) the string, producing a scratchy sound.

MUFFLED STRINGS: A percussive sound is produced by laying the fret hand across the string(s) without depressing, and striking them with the pick hand.

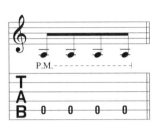

PALM MUTING: The note is partially muted by the pick hand lightly touching the string(s) just before the bridge.

RAKE: Drag the pick across the strings indicated with a single motion.

TREMOLO PICKING: The note is picked as rapidly and continuously as possible.

ARPEGGIATE: Play the notes of the chord indicated by quickly rolling them from bottom to top.

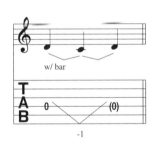

VIBRATO BAR DIVE AND RETURN: The pitch of the note or chord is dropped a specified number of steps (in rhythm) then returned to the original pitch.

VIBRATO BAR SCOOP: Depress the bar just before striking the note, then quickly release the bar.

VIBRATO BAR DIP: Strike the note and then immediately drop a specified number of steps, then release back to the original pitch.

Additional Musical Definitions

(accent) • Accentuate note (play it louder)

(accent) • Accentuate note with great intensity

(staccato) • Play the note short

⊓ • Downstroke

∨ • Upstroke

D.S. al Coda • Go back to the sign (𝄋), then play until the measure marked "***To Coda***," then skip to the section labelled "**Coda**."

D.C. al Fine • Go back to the beginning of the song and play until the measure marked "***Fine***" (end).

Rhy. Fig. • Label used to recall a recurring accompaniment pattern (usually chordal).

Riff • Label used to recall composed, melodic lines (usually single notes) which recur.

Fill • Label used to identify a brief melodic figure which is to be inserted into the arrangement.

Rhy. Fill • A chordal version of a Fill.

tacet • Instrument is silent (drops out).

• Repeat measures between signs.

• When a repeated section has different endings, play the first ending only the first time and the second ending only the second time.

NOTE: Tablature numbers in parentheses mean:
1. The note is being sustained over a system (note in standard notation is tied), or
2. The note is sustained, but a new articulation (such as a hammer-on, pull-off, slide or vibrato begins), or
3. The note is a barely audible "ghost" note (note in standard notation is also in parentheses).

THE DECADE SERIES

These collections, especially for guitarists feature the top tunes that shaped a decade transcribed note-for-note.

The 1950s

35 pivotal songs from the early rock years: All Shook Up • Be-Bop-a-Lula • Bo Diddley • Boppin' the Blues • Cannonball • Donna • Foggy Mountain Breakdown • Get Rhythm • Guita Boogie Shuffle • Heartbreak Hotel • Hound Dog • I'm Lookin' for Someone to Love • I' Movin' On • I'm Your Hoochie Coochie Man • Lonesome Town • Matchbox • Moonlight i Vermont • My Babe • Poor Little Fool • Put Your Cat Clothes On • Race With the Devil • Reb 'Rouser • Reconsider Baby • Rock Around the Clock • Rocket '88 • Rockin' Robin • Sleepwa • Slippin' and Slidin' • Susie-Q • Sweet Little Angel • Tequila • (They Call It) Stormy Monda (Stormy Monday Blues) • Wake Up Little Susie • The World Is Waiting for the Sunrise • Yanke Doodle Dixie

_____ 00690543 Guitar Recorded Versions $14.9

The 1960s

30 songs that defined the '60s: Badge • Blackbird • Fun, Fun, Fun • Gloria • Good Lovin' Green Onions • Happy Together • Hello Mary Lou • Hey Joe • Hush • I Can See for Miles • Feel Fine • I Get Around • In the Midnight Hour • Jingo (Jin-Go-Lo-Ba) • Let's Live for Toda • Louie, Louie • My Girl • Oh, Pretty Woman • On the Road Again • The Promised Land Somebody to Love • Soul Man • Suite: Judy Blue Eyes • Susie-Q • Time Is on My Side • (So Tired of Waiting for You • Train Kept A-Rollin' • Walk Don't Run • Wild Thing

_____ 00690542 Guitar Recorded Versions $14.9

The 1970s

30 top songs from the '70s: Barracuda • Best of My Love • Blue Collar Man (Long Nights) Breakdown • Burning Love • Dust in the Wind • Evil Woman • Freeway Jam • Godzilla • Happ • Landslide • Lay Down Sally • Let It Be • Maggie May • No Woman No Cry • Oye Como Va Paranoid • Rock and Roll Hoochie Koo • Show Me the Way • Smoke on the Water • So Int You • Space Oddity • Stayin' Alive • Teach Your Children • Time in a Bottle • Walk This Way Wheel in the Sky • You Ain't Seen Nothin' Yet • You Really Got Me • You've Got a Friend

_____ 00690541 Guitar Recorded Versions $15.9

The 1980s

30 songs that best represent the decade: Caught Up in You • Down Boys • 867-5309/Jenny Every Breath You Take • Eye of the Tiger • Fight for Your Right (To Party) • Heart and Soul Hit Me With Your Best Shot • I Love Rock 'N Roll • In and Out of Love • La Bamba • Land Confusion • Love Struck Baby • (Bang Your Head) Metal Health • Money for Nothing • Mon Mony • Rag Doll • Refugee • R.O.C.K. in the U.S.A. (A Salute to '60s Rock) • Rock Me • Roc You Like a Hurricane • Running on Faith • Seventeen • Start Me Up • Summer of '69 • Swe Child O' Mine • Wait • What I Like About You • Working for the Weekend • You May Be Righ

_____ 00690540 Guitar Recorded Versions $15.9

The 1990s

30 essential '90s classics: All I Wanna Do • Are You Gonna Go My Way • Barely Breathing Blue on Black • Boot Scootin' Boogie • Building a Mystery • Bulls on Parade • Come Out an Play • Cryin' • (Everything I Do) I Do It for You • Fields of Gold • Free As a Bird • Friends i Low Places • Give Me One Reason • Hold My Hand • I Can't Dance • I'm the Only One • Th Impression That I Get • Iris • Jump, Jive an' Wail • More Than Words • Santa Monica • Sem Charmed Life • Silent Lucidity • Smells Like Teen Spirit • Smooth • Tears in Heaven • Tw Princes • Under the Bridge • Wonderwall

_____ 00690539 Guitar Recorded Versions $15.9

FOR MORE INFORMATION, SEE YOUR LOCAL MUSIC DEALER, OR WRITE TO:

HAL•LEONARD®
CORPORATION
7777 W. BLUEMOUND RD. P.O. BOX 13819 MILWAUKEE, WI 53213

Prices, contents and availability subject to change without notice.

www.halleonard.com

RECORDED VERSIONS
The Best Note-For-Note Transcriptions Available

RECORDED VERSIONS GUITAR

ALL BOOKS INCLUDE TABLATURE

0016 Will Ackerman Collection	$19.95
0146 Aerosmith – Toys in the Attic	$19.95
4865 Alice In Chains – Dirt	$19.95
4932 Allman Brothers Band – Volume 1	$24.95
4933 Allman Brothers Band – Volume 2	$24.95
4934 Allman Brothers Band – Volume 3	$24.95
4877 Chet Atkins – Guitars For All Seasons	$19.95
0418 Best of Audio Adrenaline	$17.95
4918 Randy Bachman Collection	$22.95
0366 Bad Company Original Anthology - Bk 1	$19.95
0367 Bad Company Original Anthology - Bk 2	$19.95
4880 Beatles – Abbey Road	$19.95
4863 Beatles – Sgt. Pepper's Lonely Hearts Club Band	$19.95
0383 Beatles – Yellow Submarine	$19.95
0174 Beck – Mellow Gold	$17.95
0346 Beck – Mutations	$19.95
0175 Beck – Odelay	$17.95
4884 The Best of George Benson	$19.95
2385 Chuck Berry	$19.95
2200 Black Sabbath – We Sold Our Soul For Rock 'N' Roll	$19.95
0115 Blind Melon – Soup	$19.95
0305 Blink 182 – Dude Ranch	$19.95
0028 Blue Oyster Cult – Cult Classics	$19.95
0219 Blur	$19.95
0168 Roy Buchanon Collection	$19.95
0364 Cake – Songbook	$19.95
0337 Jerry Cantrell – Boggy Depot	$19.95
0293 Best of Steven Curtis Chapman	$19.95
0043 Cheap Trick – Best Of	$19.95
0171 Chicago – Definitive Guitar Collection	$22.95
0415 Clapton Chronicles – Best of Eric Clapton	$17.95
0393 Eric Clapton – Selections from Blues	$19.95
0139 Eric Clapton – Journeyman	$19.95
4869 Eric Clapton – Live Acoustic	$19.95
4896 John Mayall/Eric Clapton – Bluesbreakers	$19.95
0162 Best of the Clash	$19.95
0166 Albert Collins – The Alligator Years	$16.95
4940 Counting Crows – August & Everything After	$19.95
0197 Counting Crows – Recovering the Satellites	$19.95
4840 Cream – Disraeli Gears	$19.95
0401 Creed – Human Clay	$19.95
0352 Creed – My Own Prison	$19.95
0184 dc Talk – Jesus Freak	$19.95
0333 dc Talk – Supernatural	$19.95
0186 Alex De Grassi Guitar Collection	$19.95
0289 Best of Deep Purple	$17.95
4831 Derek And The Dominos – Layla & Other Assorted Love Songs	$19.95
0322 Ani Di Franco – Little Plastic Castle	$19.95
0187 Dire Straits – Brothers In Arms	$19.95
0191 Dire Straits – Money For Nothing	$24.95
5382 The Very Best of Dire Straits – Sultans of Swing	$19.95
0178 Willie Dixon – Master Blues Composer	$24.95
0250 Best of Duane Eddy	$16.95
0349 Eve 6	$19.95
3164 Eve 6 – Horrorscope	$19.95
0323 Fastball – All the Pain Money Can Buy	$19.95
0089 Foo Fighters	$19.95
0235 Foo Fighters – The Colour and the Shape	$19.95
0394 Foo Fighters – There Is Nothing Left to Lose	$19.95
0222 G3 Live – Satriani, Vai, Johnson	$22.95
4807 Danny Gatton – 88 Elmira St	$19.95
0438 Genesis Guitar Anthology	$19.95

00690127 Goo Goo Dolls – A Boy Named Goo	$19.95
00690338 Goo Goo Dolls – Dizzy Up the Girl	$19.95
00690117 John Gorka Collection	$19.95
00690114 Buddy Guy Collection Vol. A-J	$22.95
00690193 Buddy Guy Collection Vol. L-Y	$22.95
00694798 George Harrison Anthology	$19.95
00690068 Return Of The Hellecasters	$19.95
00692930 Jimi Hendrix – Are You Experienced?	$24.95
00692931 Jimi Hendrix – Axis: Bold As Love	$22.95
00692932 Jimi Hendrix – Electric Ladyland	$24.95
00690218 Jimi Hendrix – First Rays of the New Rising Sun	$27.95
00690038 Gary Hoey – Best Of	$19.95
00660029 Buddy Holly	$19.95
00660169 John Lee Hooker – A Blues Legend	$19.95
00690054 Hootie & The Blowfish – Cracked Rear View	$19.95
00694905 Howlin' Wolf	$19.95
00690136 Indigo Girls – 1200 Curfews	$22.95
00694938 Elmore James – Master Electric Slide Guitar	$19.95
00690167 Skip James Blues Guitar Collection	$16.95
00694833 Billy Joel For Guitar	$19.95
00694912 Eric Johnson – Ah Via Musicom	$19.95
00690169 Eric Johnson – Venus Isle	$22.95
00694799 Robert Johnson – At The Crossroads	$19.95
00693185 Judas Priest – Vintage Hits	$19.95
00690277 Best of Kansas	$19.95
00690073 B. B. King – 1950-1957	$24.95
00690098 B. B. King – 1958-1967	$24.95
00690444 B.B. King and Eric Clapton – Riding with the King	$19.95
00690134 Freddie King Collection	$17.95
00690157 Kiss – Alive	$19.95
00690163 Mark Knopfler/Chet Atkins – Neck and Neck	$19.95
00690296 Patty Larkin Songbook	$17.95
00690018 Living Colour – Best Of	$19.95
00694845 Yngwie Malmsteen – Fire And Ice	$19.95
00694956 Bob Marley – Legend	$19.95
00690283 Best of Sarah McLachlan	$19.95
00690382 Sarah McLachlan – Mirrorball	$19.95
00690354 Sarah McLachlan – Surfacing	$19.95
00690442 Matchbox 20 – Mad Season	$19.95
00690239 Matchbox 20 – Yourself or Someone Like You	$19.95
00690244 Megadeath – Cryptic Writings	$19.95
00690236 Mighty Mighty Bosstones – Let's Face It	$19.95
00690040 Steve Miller Band Greatest Hits	$19.95
00694802 Gary Moore – Still Got The Blues	$19.95
00694958 Mountain, Best Of	$19.95
00690448 MxPx – The Ever Passing Moment	$19.95
00694913 Nirvana – In Utero	$19.95
00694883 Nirvana – Nevermind	$19.95
00690026 Nirvana – Acoustic In New York	$19.95
00690121 Oasis – (What's The Story) Morning Glory	$19.95
00690204 Offspring, The – Ixnay on the Hombre	$17.95
00690203 Offspring, The – Smash	$17.95
00694830 Ozzy Osbourne – No More Tears	$19.95
00694855 Pearl Jam – Ten	$19.95
00690053 Liz Phair – Whip Smart	$19.95
00690176 Phish – Billy Breathes	$22.95
00690424 Phish – Farmhouse	$19.95
00690331 Phish – The Story of Ghost	$19.95
00690428 Pink Floyd – Dark Side of the Moon	$19.95
00693800 Pink Floyd – Early Classics	$19.95
00690456 P.O.D. – The Fundamental Elements of Southtown	$19.95
00694967 Police – Message In A Box Boxed Set	$70.00
00694974 Queen – A Night At The Opera	$19.95

00690395 Rage Against The Machine – The Battle of Los Angeles	$19.95
00690145 Rage Against The Machine – Evil Empire	$19.95
00690179 Rancid – And Out Come the Wolves	$22.95
00690055 Red Hot Chili Peppers – Bloodsugarsexmagik	$19.95
00690379 Red Hot Chili Peppers – Californication	$19.95
00690090 Red Hot Chili Peppers – One Hot Minute	$22.95
00694937 Jimmy Reed – Master Bluesman	$19.95
00694899 R.E.M. – Automatic For The People	$19.95
00690260 Jimmie Rodgers Guitar Collection	$19.95
00690014 Rolling Stones – Exile On Main Street	$24.95
00690186 Rolling Stones – Rock & Roll Circus	$19.95
00690135 Otis Rush Collection	$19.95
00690031 Santana's Greatest Hits	$19.95
00690150 Son Seals – Bad Axe Blues	$17.95
00690128 Seven Mary Three – American Standards	$19.95
00120105 Kenny Wayne Shepherd – Ledbetter Heights	$19.95
00120123 Kenny Wayne Shepherd – Trouble Is	$19.95
00690196 Silverchair – Freak Show	$19.95
00690130 Silverchair – Frogstomp	$19.95
00690041 Smithereens – Best Of	$19.95
00690385 Sonicflood	$19.95
00694885 Spin Doctors – Pocket Full Of Kryptonite	$19.95
00694921 Steppenwolf, The Best Of	$22.95
00694957 Rod Stewart – Acoustic Live	$22.95
00690021 Sting – Fields Of Gold	$19.95
00690242 Suede – Coming Up	$19.95
00694824 Best Of James Taylor	$16.95
00690238 Third Eye Blind	$19.95
00690403 Third Eye Blind – Blue	$19.95
00690267 311	$19.95
00690030 Toad The Wet Sprocket	$19.95
00690228 Tonic – Lemon Parade	$19.95
00690295 Tool – Aenima	$19.95
00690039 Steve Vai – Alien Love Secrets	$24.95
00690172 Steve Vai – Fire Garden	$24.95
00690023 Jimmie Vaughan – Strange Pleasures	$19.95
00690370 Stevie Ray Vaughan and Double Trouble – The Real Deal: Greatest Hits Volume 2	$22.95
00690455 Stevie Ray Vaughan – Blues at Sunrise	$19.95
00660136 Stevie Ray Vaughan – In Step	$19.95
00690417 Stevie Ray Vaughan – Live at Carnegie Hall	$19.95
00694835 Stevie Ray Vaughan – The Sky Is Crying	$19.95
00694776 Vaughan Brothers – Family Style	$19.95
00120026 Joe Walsh – Look What I Did...	$24.95
00694789 Muddy Waters – Deep Blues	$24.95
00690071 Weezer	$19.95
00690286 Weezer – Pinkerton	$19.95
00690447 Who, The – Best of	$24.95
00694970 Who, The – Definitive Collection A-E	$24.95
00694971 Who, The – Definitive Collection F-Li	$24.95
00694972 Who, The – Definitive Collection Lo-R	$24.95
00694973 Who, The – Definitive Collection S-Y	$24.95
00690319 Stevie Wonder Hits	$17.95

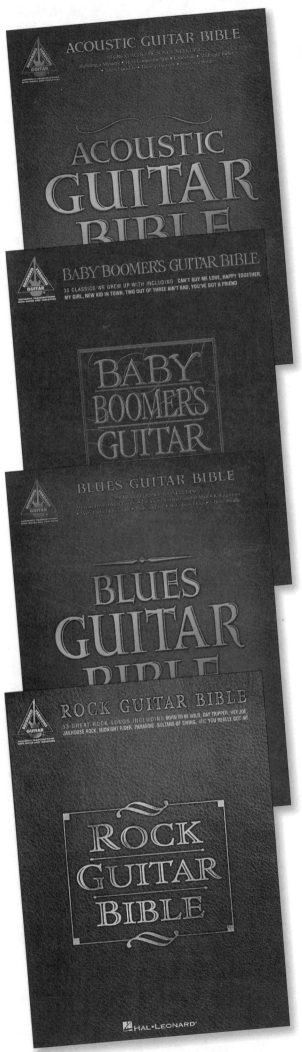

GUITAR BIBLES

from

HAL·LEONARD®

Hal Leonard proudly presents the Guitar Bible series. Each volume contains best-selling songs in authentic, note-for-note transcriptions with notes and tablature. $19.95 each

ACOUSTIC GUITAR BIBLE

35 essential classics for those who prefer acoustic guitar. Songs include: Angie • Building a Mystery • Change the World • Dust in the Wind • Here Comes the Sun • Hold My Hand • Iris • Leaving on a Jet Plane • Maggie May • The Man Who Sold the World • Southern Cross • Tears in Heaven • Wild World • You Were Meant for Me • and more.
_____00690432

BABY BOOMER'S GUITAR BIBLE

Note-for-note transcriptions for 35 crown-jewel classics from rock 'n' roll's greatest era. Includes: Angie • Can't Buy Me Love • Happy Together • Hey Jude • I Heard It Through the Grapevine • Imagine • It's Still Rock and Roll to Me • Laughing • Longer • My Girl • New Kid in Town • Rebel, Rebel • Two Out of Three Ain't Bad • Wild Thing • Wonderful Tonight • and more.
_____00690412

BLUES GUITAR BIBLE

The only book of the blues you need. 35 exact transcriptions of such classics as: All Your Love (I Miss Loving) • Boom Boom • Everyday (I Have the Blues) • Hide Away • I Can't Quit You Baby • I'm Your Hoochie Coochie Man • Killing Floor • Kind Hearted Woman Blues • Mary Had a Little Lamb • Pride and Joy • Sweet Little Angel • The Things That I Used to Do • The Thrill Is Gone • and more.
_____00690437

BLUES-ROCK GUITAR BIBLE

The definitive collection of 35 note-for-note guitar transcriptions, including: Bad Love • Black Hearted Woman • Blue on Black • Boom Boom (Out Go the Lights) • Couldn't Stand the Weather • Cross Road Blues (Crossroads) • Hide Away • The House Is Rockin' • Killing Floor • Love Struck Baby • Move It on Over • Piece of My Heart • Statesboro Blues • Still Got the Blues • Train Kept a Rollin' • You Shook Me • and more.
_____00690450

COUNTRY GUITAR BIBLE

35 revered country classics in one hefty collection, including: Ain't Goin' Down ('Til the Sun Comes Up) • Blue Eyes Crying in the Rain • Boot Scootin' Boogie • Friends in Low Places • I'm So Lonesome I Could Cry • My Baby Thinks He's a Train • T-R-O-U-B-L-E • and more.
_____00690465

FOLK-ROCK GUITAR BIBLE

35 essential folk-rock guitar favorites, including: At Seventeen • Blackbird • Do You Believe in Magic • Fire and Rain • Happy Together • Here Comes the Sun • Leaving on a Jet Plane • Me and Bobby McGee • Our House • Time in a Bottle • Turn! Turn! Turn! (To Everything There Is a Season) • You've Got a Friend • and more.
_____00690464

HARD ROCK GUITAR BIBLE

The essential collection of 35 hard rock classics, including: Back in the Saddle • Ballroom Blitz • Bang a Gong (Get It On) • Barracuda • Fight the Good Fight • Hair of the Dog • Living After Midnight • Rock You like a Hurricane • School's Out • Stone Cold Crazy • War Pigs • Welcome to the Jungle • You Give Love a Bad Name • and more.
_____00690453

JAZZ GUITAR BIBLE

The one book that has all of the jazz guitar classics transcribed note-for-note, with standard notation and tablature. Includes over 30 songs: Body and Soul • Girl Talk • I'll Remember April • In a Sentimental Mood • My Funny Valentine • Nuages • Satin Doll • So What • Star Dust • Take Five • Tangerine • Yardbird Suite • and more.
_____00690466

R&B GUITAR BIBLE

A divine collection of 35 R&B classics, including: Brick House • Dancing in the Street • Fire • I Can't Help Myself (Sugar Pie, Honey Bunch) • I Got You (I Feel Good) • I Heard It Through the Grapevine • Love Rollercoaster • My Girl • Papa's Got a Brand New Bag • Shining Star • Sir Duke • Super Freak • (Your Love Keeps Lifting Me) Higher and Higher • and more.
_____00690452

ROCK GUITAR BIBLE

Exact transcriptions in notes and tab of 33 essential rock songs: All Day and All of the Night • Born to Be Wild • Day Tripper • Gloria • Hey Joe • Jailhouse Rock • Midnight Rider • Money • Paranoid • Sultans of Swing • Walk This Way • You Really Got Me • more!
_____00690313

FOR MORE INFORMATION, SEE YOUR LOCAL MUSIC DEALER, OR WRITE TO:

HAL·LEONARD® CORPORATION
7777 W. BLUEMOUND RD. P.O. BOX 13819 MILWAUKEE, WI 53213

Prices, contents, and availability subject to change without notice.

www.halleonard.com

0101